Praise for

HE WANTED THE MOON

"The text of Dr. Baird's manuscript is haunting. The tone is one a suspense writer might struggle to sustain: The most unreliable of narrators, Dr. Baird is objective, charming, humorous, then suddenly just a little off, and then flat-out gone, leaving an irrational stranger in his place. The reader can almost watch the circuits in his brain surge and dim just as, Ms. Baird reports, the handwriting in the manuscript morphed from disciplined to disorderly and back again."

—*New York Times*

"Perry Baird emerges as thoughtful and at times eerily aware of his condition as well as his inability to elude either its symptoms or the primitive treatments for them. . . . The elder Baird's narrative is cinematic, featuring Ratched-like nurses and an escape scene straight out of *The Fugitive*. . . . [Dr. Baird] never really knew his daughter—or her achievement in telling this story."

—*Washington Post*

"Baird's lonely, angry, grief-stricken, and occasionally grandiose account of his illness and its shattering costs is the reason we can't put [this book] down. His sharply detailed recollections are sometimes sane and sometimes not, but his writing is lucid even when his thinking isn't. His manuscript is a plea to understand his experience and, by extension, others'."

—*Boston Globe*

"*He Wanted the Moon* is one of the most disturbing and profoundly moving books I've read in years, and one of the great father-daughter books of our time. . . . The brilliant Dr. Perry

Baird's memoir lets you see up close what it is like to go through the most manic phases of bipolar disorder—it is a nightmare, but this book is a damn wonder. Through it, Mimi Baird has finally given her father the credit he was due."

—PAT CONROY, author of *The Prince of Tides* and *The Death of Santini*

"Powerful, fascinating, and completely unique. This heartbreaking book is a one-of-a-kind first person window into the world of psychiatric illness before the era of drug therapies in this country. Reading *He Wanted the Moon* is a bit like discovering the Dead Sea Scrolls—it is one of the most eloquent, powerful, and important accounts of mental illness ever put to paper."

—DAVID ISAY, founder of StoryCorps and author of *Listening Is an Act of Love* and *Ties That Bind*

"Thanks to a daughter's brave determination to excavate her absentee father's life, we are gifted with deep personal insight into a brilliant but sick mind that could have been lost forever. This is a truly important book—a devastatingly honest account of mental illness that provides personal insight into long-ranging travesties of psychiatric care in the U.S. Unforgettable."

—SUSANNAH CAHALAN, author of *Brain on Fire*

"Dr. Perry Baird's vivid account of his own madness, and the treatment he received, is as remarkable as it is disturbing. By sharing her family's story, Mimi Baird has certainly done a great service to her father's memory. But she's also made a significant contribution to the literature of mental health. *He Wanted the Moon* is a poignant book, and, I believe, an important one."

—ALEXANDRA STYRON, author of *Reading My Father*

"*He Wanted the Moon* does for mental illness what *The Immortal Life of Henrietta Lacks* did for the science of cancer: at once reveal suffering and heal it through knowledge. By allowing her father to be heard, Mimi Baird gives voices to all Americans silenced by mental illness down the decades. A miraculous story told in a miracle of a book."

—AMITY SHLAES, author of *Coolidge* and *The Forgotten Man*

"Here is how you know you have just read a wonderful book: You immediately begin telling everybody you know about it, which is exactly what I did when I finished *He Wanted the Moon*."

—ROBERT WHITAKER, author of *Anatomy of an Epidemic* and *Mad in America*

"*He Wanted the Moon* details the horrendous treatment commonly given to patients at a time when there was no known way of ameliorating the dangerous and self-destructive behavior that often characterizes manic depression. This is a fascinating and informative book which I would highly recommend."

—DR. ELLIOT VALENSTEIN, professor emeritus of psychology and neuroscience at the University of Michigan and author of *Blaming the Brain*

"Mimi Baird's short book about her father's long struggle with mental illness is a tale within a tale. She longed to know why he had simply disappeared one day from her life, and what she found was his own vivid account of watching himself slide into darkness. Mimi has performed a quiet miracle, giving life back to a man everyone wanted to forget."

—THOMAS POWERS, Pulitzer Prize winner and author of *The Killing of Crazy Horse*

"Astonishing in its illuminations . . . This striking and poignant family story evokes compassion for everyone affected by this cruel malady."

—*Booklist*

"Through this moving memoir, Baird slowly brings her father back to life and reveals the sordid history of treating mental illness."

—*Bookpage*

"Perry Baird was a pioneer in attempting to understand the workings of manic depression. . . . In bringing her father's harrowing, tragic, and moving story to life, Mimi Baird celebrates him and gives voice to the terrible suffering the mentally ill once endured, and still do today, and challenges the prejudices and misperceptions the public continues to have about the disease."

—*Publishers Weekly*

"Moving . . . [Baird] sketches the life of a man who had done brilliantly in college and medical school—even coauthoring a paper with the eminent physiologist Walter Cannon—but who would be felled by psychosis. . . . A sobering account of how little we knew and how much we still have to learn about mental illness—especially how not to treat it."

—*Kirkus Reviews*

HE WANTED THE MOON

8/8/18

to Jean
Mike's golf
Partner —

Mimi Baird

These days of constant
_____ were the darkest of
_____ life _____
_____
_____
_____

_____ filled with hatred. When
_____ brought back, the stra
_____ was removed & there
a pack already laid for
_____. I looked into a corner
said:
"It seems to me that I.

HE WANTED THE MOON

THE MADNESS AND MEDICAL GENIUS OF DR. PERRY BAIRD, AND HIS DAUGHTER'S QUEST TO KNOW HIM

MIMI BAIRD

WITH EVE CLAXTON

B\D\W\Y
BROADWAY BOOKS
NEW YORK

Library of Congress Cataloging-in-Publication Data
Baird, Mimi.
    He wanted the moon : the madness and medical genius
 of Dr. Perry Baird, and his daughter's quest to know him /
 Mimi Baird ; with Eve Claxton.
        pages cm
    1. Baird, Perry—Mental health. 2. Manic-depressive
persons—United States—Biography. 3. Manic-depressive
illness—United States—History. 4. Physicians—United
States—Biography. I. Claxton, Eve. II. Title.
    RC516.B34   2015
    616.89'50092—dc23
    [B]   2014012743

ISBN 978-0-8041-3749-2
eBook ISBN 978-0-8041-3748-5

Printed in the United States of America

Book design by Barbara Sturman
Cover design by Elena Giavaldi
Cover photograph: Courtesy of Mimi Baird

10 9 8 7 6 5 4 3 2 1

First Paperback Edition

To my two children

JAKE AND MEG

the pearls of my life

Author's Note

This book is the culmination of many years collecting and assembling materials relating to my father, Dr. Perry Cossart Baird Jr. (Throughout this book, for brevity's sake, we refer to him as Dr. Perry Baird.)

Included here is my father's original manuscript from 1944, as well as excerpts from his medical records and from letters he wrote and received.

Readers should be aware that we have edited his manuscript—and the other original materials—in order to improve readability. Any amendments made were in the interests of consistency and clarity. In some places, spellings, tenses, and usage have changed and a word or two added for intelligibility. We have not used brackets to indicate these changes.

My father's writing work was repeatedly interrupted by his illness, and his original manuscript includes more than one draft in some sections (as well as passages unrelated to his stay at Westborough). We have distilled or trimmed the text in these instances for the sake of concision. We have not used ellipses to indicate where lines have been deleted.

Throughout, we have been mindful to preserve the tone and meaning—and sometimes lack of clear meaning due to my father's mental state—of the original writing. No names have been changed; no characters or events have been invented; no full sentences have been added.

Our goal has been to fulfill my father's wish: "to complete the job in the right way."

With Earth's first Clay they did the Last Man knead
And there of the Last Harvest sow'd the Seed
And the first Morning of Creation wrote
What the Last Dawn of Reckoning Shall read.

Yesterday, This Day's Madness did Prepare;
To-Morrow's Silence, Triumph, or Despair:
Drink! For you know not whence you came, or why:
Drink! For you know not why you go, nor where.

—*The Rubáiyát of Omar Khayyám*

PART I

ECHOES FROM A

DUNGEON CELL

PROLOGUE

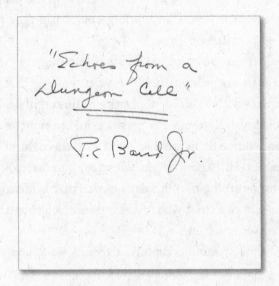

It was the spring of 1994 when I returned from work to find the package containing my father's manuscript on my door-step. I was fifty-six years old and I'd been waiting for some word of him for most of my life.

I was a six-year-old child when he stopped coming home. My mother refused to say where he had gone, except to tell me that he was "ill" and "away." That same year of 1944, she filed for a divorce and quickly remarried, closing the chapter of her life that included my father. I was never taken to visit him growing up; his name was rarely mentioned in our house. Since childhood, I had been informed in fleeting comments that he suffered from manic depression. I had seen him again only once, very briefly, before his death in 1959.

The late-afternoon light cast long, sharp shadows across my entranceway and the box on the step. For decades my father's manuscript had been kept in an old briefcase in the garage of a family member in Texas, all but forgotten. I had only recently learned of its existence.

I picked up the carton and carefully brought it inside. I knew so little about my father, Perry Baird—only that he had been a doctor with a successful practice in Boston in his heyday. Yet I could vividly recall his presence in my early years: the gleaming white coat he wore at his offices, the sight of him at the Chestnut Hill train station where my mother took me to greet him, returning from his day's work. After he disappeared, I felt the pain of a child who misses a parent, a feeling that had never completely left me.

My hands trembling slightly, I took a knife and made a slit along the packing tape on top of the carton. Opening the flaps, I peered inside, glimpsing handwriting on the top sheaf. Cautiously—as if my father's words might bite—I took a piece of the paper between my thumb and forefinger. It was creamy and slightly translucent, of the onionskin kind used for making carbon copies in the days of the typewriter. I could see that it was covered in many lines of penciled script.

I quickly put the page back and closed the carton. After fifty years of silence, it was going to take me a little while to work up the courage to hear from him again.

Some days later, I reopened the box, this time pulling out a handful of pages, then another. Soon, the stack on my kitchen counter was over a foot high. I attempted to read my father's words, but it was impossible to connect the sentences on one page with the next. Further investigation revealed that the papers had been shuffled out of order. After much searching, I located what appeared to be a title written in bold strokes: "Echoes from a Dungeon Cell."

It took many months to restore the manuscript to some semblance of order. As I rearranged the pages, I realized that these were my father's memoirs. For the first time, I learned what had happened to him all those years ago. He had not vanished (as I had sometimes suspected as a child). He had not left us. He had been removed against his will to Westborough State Hospital, a psychiatric institution just outside Boston, where he had written about his experiences on the papers I held in my hands. My father was afflicted with a severe mental illness during a period before any effective treatment existed, many years before the advent of modern psychiatric medications. Like hundreds of thousands of mentally ill patients at that time, he was a victim of both his disease and the stigma surrounding it. He was shut away, institutionalized, his family advised to try to forget him, an edict my mother did her best to follow.

The arrival of the manuscript in my life marked the beginning of a long journey to know my father. Along with the other traces I have found of him—in letters, his published articles, his medical records, and photographs—I was able to discover not only a father, but a writer and a scientist, a man whose insights were extraordinarily advanced for his times.

Although *Echoes from a Dungeon Cell* was never published in my father's lifetime, it was his great hope that it would one day find publication. In letters written after he departed West-borough, he explained:

Last year when I was ill, I went through a series of adventures both colorful and painful. At that time I was asked to write the story of some of my strange travels and so, out of the cauldron of despair, came forth my manuscript. It is a long-continued account of every kind of suffering and disaster—February 20 to July 8, 1944. By going along slowly, depicting in detail the intricate succession of events, perhaps I can unravel and clarify the sequence of events and the relative importance of the various connecting links and contributing episodes . . .

I believe that the inadequate understanding of manic-depression as displayed by friends and relatives imposes unnecessary hardships on the manic-depressive. I have read widely about manic depression, I have lived through five prolonged sui-cidal depressions, four acute manic episodes and many hypo-manic phases. I have learned by expe-rience how all the treatments feel: straight-jackets, wristlets, anklets, paraldehyde injections, hot and cold packs, continuous tub, close confinement to small spaces, and all the many inventions that man has created for the manic-psychosis. As a patient, I have studied many other patients at four psycho-pathic hospitals, including one city and one state hospital.

Out of my recent agonies came a dauntless

furor scribendi and I have written a very readable book. It is my conviction and I know you'll agree that artistic creativeness finds its best expression after it has been fashioned by the agonies and tortures that life imposes.

CHAPTER ONE

When my father's manuscript begins, he is forty years old and has lived with the diagnosis of manic depression for more than ten years. By now, he knows very well the symptoms of his disease, its dangerous, ecstatic highs followed by pitch-dark depressions. It is February 1944, and he has retreated to the Ritz-Carlton Hotel in Boston, as he often did when he felt himself becoming manic, in order to protect his family from his increasingly erratic behavior.

▲

Dr. Perry Baird at the Ritz-Carlton Hotel, Boston

Although he had informed my mother that he was going to the Ritz to work on his book, he soon became distracted from his work. My sister, Catherine, and I stayed with our mother in Chestnut Hill, just outside the city, oblivious to events unfolding around us.

> *Why so much happiness in the manic state? Perhaps an ability to dwell upon only the Pleasing tho...*

THE morning of February 20, 1944, I slept deeply but awoke at the Ritz after only three or four hours of sleep, feeling that strange manic exuberance. I bathed, shaved and dressed, had breakfast, and then started out for a walk across the Boston Public Gardens. I ran short distances and leaped wildly over the broad flowerbeds. Anyone who might have seen me from the hotel would have thought my behavior a little unrestrained. I felt wonderful but restless, feverishly overactive, impatient. After walking for about ten minutes, I located a taxi and drove to my home in Chestnut Hill. I felt possessed with demoniacal energy. I was acutely manic.

When I arrived at my home, no one seemed to be there. I wandered around to the backyard and on impulse, climbed over the twelve-foot wire fence surrounding the deer park. I broke into a run. As I ran up and over an elevation of land in the deer park I saw a group of deer standing in the clearing. I wondered if I could run as fast as a deer and if I could catch one. I increased my pace by a sudden burst of speed. All of the deer except one turned and ran. This one deer stood her ground a few moments, wagging her funny little short white tail. Then she too turned and ran away. I hid behind a large boulder, and as the deer ran around in a circle they came past the boulder, and once again I tried to overtake them. The small herd of deer was led by a large stag that, as I jumped into his path, might have turned upon me, guided by his protective interest. Instead, he merely led his flock around me and they soon outdistanced me.

After wandering around the deer park for a while and finding all the gates locked, I climbed back over the fence and went into the back door of my house. I found Nona, our maid, sitting at a table, her head in the crook of her arm, evidently crying. She must have known I felt upset. I went through the kitchen hurriedly, going into the dining room and through the living room, then out the front door.

As I walked along without my topcoat or overcoat, I felt quite hot even though it was a rather cold day. The sun was shining brightly. I looked into the sun but was not dazzled by its glare. Soon, the sun changed its appearance. It was gradually transformed from a fuzzy ball of fire with a shapely outline into a round silver-like disc with a clear halo around it. I looked away from the sun and, as my eyes turned upon the snow in front of me, I could see smoothly outlined, deep yellow spots upon the snow.

Soon, I arrived at the home of my good friend, the psychiatrist Dr. Reginald Smithwick. I walked across his lawn; then I stopped at his living room window. As was usual for him on Sunday morning, he was sitting in his armchair by the side of the fire, working on tables and texts of a scientific paper. I knocked and, without waiting long, went in.

"Good morning, Reg," I said.

"Hi, Perry," he replied. "Come and sit down."

I sat on the sofa and then lay down for a moment. I cannot recall the context of our conversation, but I admitted that I was somewhat manic and spoke of a feeling of greatly augmented physical strength. Saying this, I rose from my position, walked across the room, and picked up a poker by the fireplace. It was an iron instrument with a shiny copper sheath.

"Just as an experiment, let me see if I can bend this poker into a figure eight or a bow knot," I said.

I started to twist the poker.

"Don't!" Reg said in a high-pitched and nervous voice, as if some important decision rested upon what was about to transpire. Paying little attention to what might have been interpreted as a very important warning, I went ahead and twisted the copper poker into the shape of a double circle.

I could see that Reg was a little upset.

"Will you call me a taxi?" I asked.

Obligingly he went to the telephone immediately and called me a taxi.

"Please take me to the Ritz hotel," I said to the driver.

As we drove to the Ritz, it seemed to me that the streets were singularly deserted for a fairly advanced hour of Sunday morning. When the taxi pulled up in front of the Ritz there was no other car in sight.

In the far corner of the lobby, one of my secretaries, Charlotte Richards, was waiting. I had called my office earlier and asked for someone to come. Charlotte seemed quite nervous.

We stepped into the elevator and went to my room. There was another luscious copper and iron poker by the fireplace. I picked it up and went into my steel-bending performance.

"I am the only one who would come," Charlotte commented. "The rest were afraid."

During the following two hours or so, I dictated large amounts to Charlotte, drank enormous quantities of Coca Cola, and smoked Kool cigarettes almost constantly. The waiter brought up Coca Cola by the dozen bottles. I believe that the combination of Coca Colas and Kool cigarettes aggravated my state of excitation. My thoughts seemed to travel with the speed and clearness of light. I dictated and talked continuously.

Why so much happiness in the manic state? Perhaps an ability to dwell upon only the pleasing phases of one's past experiences and current problems, combined with an ability to shut out disturbing considerations; the process of thought seems not only clear and logical but powerful and penetrating, features made possible by focusing all attention upon the major facts, leaving out distracting details. Perhaps the euphoria is also in part physiological in nature, representing a spastic sudden flushing of areas of the vascular-bed long idle but now overactive; the escape is a transition from long phases of inactivity to a state characterized by an easy and abundant flow of energy.

The phone rang in the bedroom. It was my wife, Gretta.

"Good morning, Perry, how are you?" she asked.

"Oh, just fine, dear," I replied. "How are you? I'm here giving some dictation to Charlotte."

"Dr. Lang wants you to call him," Gretta informed me.

At this point I should have had every reason to realize the hazardous nature of my position. A call from Dr. Lang—the superintendent of Westborough State Hospital—should have indicated the possibility of my return to that psychiatric institution, a prospect that had long filled me with a sense of miserable apprehension.

In my wallet, I had about six hundred dollars. I could have walked out of my room on the pretext of going to the drug store and could have managed to get out of the state. If I had done so, I might have saved myself months of grief and despair. But—by some cruel stroke of fate, by some strange absence of any sense of caution—I went right on with what I was doing, paying slight heed to the dark cloud hanging low over me.

At my request, Charlotte called Dr. Reg Smithwick and asked him to see whether he could get a room at Massachusetts General Hospital for a few days of careful chemical studies of blood and urine. There were no rooms available.

As I dictated to Charlotte, I began collecting urine specimens in empty Coca Cola bottles, placing the specimens on the window ledge to keep them cool. I recall that the output of urine was quite large and seemed to be controlled by thought and emotion. When pleasurable ideas came to mind, I could seem to feel my bladder filling up. But when I felt anxiety, the flow of urine seemed to cease. I wonder whether the renal arteries and arterioles were expanding and contracting under the influence of nervous stress and nervous relaxation.

During these activities I made occasional trips to the bathroom and rubbed olive oil into my skin and hair. For some weeks my hair had been exceedingly dry, so much so that it would not stay in place after being combed and showed a tendency to stick up in all directions. It looked and felt like straw. This condition had developed at the end of a three- or four-month period of time during which I had followed a successful weight-reducing program cutting out all butter. Though I had continued to consume cod liver oil capsules containing vitamin A, this source did not evidently replace the loss from omission of butter. I feel sure that I was suffering from real vitamin A deficiency.

My food arrived. I had ordered an enormous meal consisting of about six eggs, two steaks and other items. My behavior was certainly unrestrained, to say the least. Charlotte left.

Soon after, my wife Gretta arrived with the children. She remained standing and began to make preparation to leave almost immediately after arriving.

Our eldest daughter, Mimi, was standing near me.

"I want to stay with Daddy," she said.

Instantly, Gretta found some excuse for taking Mimi with her and they left. Gretta's final remark was that they were going to The Country Club to skate.

I went to the bar, consuming another Coca Cola. I decided to follow Gretta to The Country Club and went out to get a taxi. At The Country Club, I walked towards the skating pond, but I couldn't find Gretta and the children and so returned to the clubhouse. As I came to the door, they were just leaving.

"I'll come back for you," Gretta said.

"Don't bother," I replied.

Gretta left to go home; I remained to face the tragedy of a lifetime.

Inside the clubhouse, I sat on the large divan looking out over the racetrack and golf course, and ordered a Coca Cola. The large old majestic trees and vast expanse of snow-covered lawn that can be seen from the side of the club-house form a beautiful and restful view. Very few people were around. I went over and spoke to a few friends. One of them refused to have a drink with me. (Could he have known that I was trying to keep my promise to my psychiatrist not to drink?) He acted a little strangely. Later he departed.

I ordered a martini that I sipped slowly. At this stage of events other friends began to file in, including Storer Baldwin, who walked up to me in a friendly manner, shaking my hand.

"Hello," he said.

I rose and spoke to him.

"I hate you!" I added softly.

Storer looked at me in rather a strange manner.

"That's pleasant," he said.

I heard someone say that Storer had ordered tea. I looked over his way, and to my astonishment, he was sitting before the fireplace with a tray of tea and sandwiches before him and surrounded by his customary group of friends and their children.

As if in a trance, I walked over to Storer, and watched him drink tea. I looked around and said hello to some of my friends. I laid my half empty martini glass on Storer's tray and walked away.

The President of the Massachusetts Medical Society, Dr. Channing Frothingham, and his wife came into the room.

I sat down with Dr. and Mrs. Frothingham and talked with them for a few minutes. Dr. Frothingham invited me to have a drink with them and to eat with them. I felt greatly honored because I have always admired Dr. Frothingham. I recall discussing court tennis, at which Dr. Frothingham had been a world champion. I made some sort of a boast that I thought I could beat him (manic overconfidence). I hope the remark sounded humorous.

A boy came along and said that someone wanted me at the front. Completely innocent of the nature of this call, I walked out of the living room and down the corridor. I recognized plain-clothes policemen—three of them standing at the front desk near the telephone operator. By now, it was too late to retrace my steps. I walked into the midst of them and soon verified my suspicions: they had come to take me to Westborough State Hospital.

I knew that I needed help. I felt a desperate desire to escape the horror of returning to a psychiatric institution. I went to the club telephone booth and began to call my psychiatrist friends but they were not at home. I reached our family physician, Dr. Porter, and told him what was about to happen. I asked him to help me.

"It's up to you, my boy," he said.

What could he have meant by this statement?

I might have thought to call my lawyer, but I didn't. Finally I called Dr. Lang, Superintendent of Westborough Hospital.

"I think you'd better come on out," Lang said dryly.

I left the telephone booth.

"There's no hurry, Doctor," said the policeman in charge.

"Please excuse me," I replied. "I'd like to go back and speak to my friend, Dr. Frothingham."

I went back into the living room and found that Dr. and Mrs. Frothingham had gone into the dining room. I went to their table and drew up a chair.

"They have come to take me back to Westborough," I said in a voice that was soft but which must have betrayed my despair.

Mrs. Frothingham sat very quietly, saying nothing, but looking very tense.

I walked into the living room and found our Chestnut Hill neighbor, Helen Webster, sitting with a group of guests. To my own surprise I went over and sat close to her, placing my head on her shoulder. Her friends looked surprised. She rose immediately and took me by the arm.

Helen and I walked to the entrance to the men's bar and stood there alone for a moment.

"Will you kiss me, Helen?" I asked.

Helen came up to me and kissed me very softly on the cheek and left.

Dr. Frothingham and a group of Club members came down the hallway with the policemen.

"All of Perry's troubles are sexual," said Dr. Frothingham as he walked into the bar.

I looked around at the many people surrounding me. Suddenly three state troopers came into the room and stood at the edge of the crowd.

I was standing with my hands behind my back. The plain-clothes policeman slipped a pair of handcuffs on my wrists. I felt him doing it. I did not resist. Suddenly, two policemen raised me into the air, assisted by two club members. I held my body stiff. I closed my eyes. I was lowered to my feet at the door of a state police patrol car and slipped into the backseat. Two state police officers stepped in and sat down, one on each side of me. Two other state policemen sat in the front seat. We drove away.

And so the wheel of fortune turns slowly round and round and stops here for a bit of success or happiness and again for other dictates of circumstance.

I am caught, caught, caught.

CHAPTER TWO

The state troopers who apprehended my father at The Country Club drove him immediately to Westborough State Hospital, a thirty-mile distance. This was not my father's first visit to a mental institution. By 1944, he had already been held at three other hospitals during past manic breaks, in addition to a stay at Westborough the previous year. In the course of each hospital visit, his doctors kept detailed medical records, so that on his readmittance in February of 1944, the following notes on his life and medical history were readily available:

Westborough State Hospital, Massachusetts, 1944

The patient was born in Mexia, Texas, July 8, 1903, after a very difficult labor by forceps. Early development seemed entirely normal. He began life as an extremely energetic, self-confident, rather aggressive child. He bit his nails and was afraid of dogs, but no other neurotic traits were ascertained.

The patient started school at six. He always seemed rather precocious mentally, but because of his extreme energy and over-activity, he was not particularly studious as a child. It was difficult to make him understand that he had to study and he failed in the First Grade. He was chastised by his father, which consisted one

night of an almost continuous two-hour beating.
After this, he became a good student.

The patient's father was a brilliant, domi-
neering and powerful character who was easily
angered and susceptible to mood swings. He was
not liked but respected by everyone. The father
had had a nervous breakdown as a young man, type
unknown. The father's profession was dentist.
The mother was described as a sensitive, stable,
self-sacrificing, sweet and lovable person.

When the boy was ten, the father felt he had
broken his spirit so he changed his tactics and
encouraged him to fight back and show spirit. The
patient rapidly developed into an aggressive and
self-reliant person and became a natural leader.
He also became conscious of mood fluctuations.

In high school, the patient was head of the
class and graduated an honor man. He graduated
from the University of Texas at the age of 21 in
1924 a Phi Beta Kappa. He entered Harvard Medical
School that fall. At Harvard, he never did anything socially but spent all his time in study.
He slept little and worked much. His associates
and classmates admired him for his outstanding
brilliance.

He never underestimated himself. He published a paper while still an undergraduate and,
during his last year, he taught freshman physiology. In 1928 he had the distinction of graduating
from Harvard Medical School, magna cum laude. He
had his internship at Ann Arbor for two years,
where he was an instructor. Following this he
was a resident for two years at Massachusetts

General Hospital. He did unusually well in both positions.

The patient met his wife in January 1931 and married her after a ten-month courtship. At the time, he was 29 and she was 21. He described his wife as a beautiful woman, with a natural endowment of personality and character. His married life was very happy except that his wife initially did not wish to have children for fear there would be insanity, since her father had had several depressive attacks. The patient and his wife were sexually well adjusted.

In 1932 he accepted a Harvard Fellowship to study skin diseases with Dr. John Stokes in Philadelphia. He was doing exceedingly well until he had his first manic attack in December 1932. He had been working on a paper and sent it to his associates in Boston for their comment. When the manuscript was returned and many changes were made, the patient felt indignant. He decided to write a fictional short story that he talked about incessantly and could not keep off his mind. He wrote the whole story, except for details, within 24 hours. He was so sure that he could sell this story, that on receiving his salary, he spent the entire amount. He thought that he had cures for various ailments, refused to eat anything, and would only drink milk. He could not sleep, became extremely irritable, threatening and pugnacious. He begged his wife not to cross him in any way.

After a whole week without sleep, he left Philadelphia for New York City to see about

publishing this story. While in New York he
had bought many clothes, which he did not need,
rode about in taxis, which was most unusual for
him. While in New York he met a physician friend
whom he had known in Boston, who recognized the
patient's excited condition and had him return
to Philadelphia.

The patient was sent to the Philadelphia
Hospital for Mental and Nervous Diseases and
remained there twenty-five days. Here he showed
extreme mental over-activity. His speech was
rapid but distinct, as was his mood. He was vol-
uble and over-productive. He made many gestures
and with some facial grimacing. He climbed over
the furniture and jumped on the piano to examine
a clock. He insisted on climbing several trees
and a flagpole while out on a walk. On another
occasion, he picked up a table and threw it away
from him in a burst of energy.

At first, he was fairly coherent. He talked
principally about his paper and occasionally got
fairly far afield and often did not pursue the
discussion through to its completion. Several
days later, he was far more distractible and
broke off in the midst of explaining some matter
and spoke about something he noticed on the wall.
He played one piece on the piano over and over
again, explaining that he was using the music to
interpret his past activities.

At times he was very irritable and threatening to anyone's interfering with what he wanted
to do. He felt that there were crowds of people
about the hospital who had heard that he was
there and were trying to get in to look at the

person who had made such wonderful discoveries. He showed considerable insight into his condition and said that he knew that he was "manic." He said he recognized the hospital was the best place for him. At other times, he denied this. He said that at one time when he became very much excited he had had delusions and hallucinations, but that these were just a product of his excited and confused states at these times.

One week after admission, it was decided to give him Narcosis treatment by means of sodium amytal. The matter was explained to the patient and he agreed at once and asked that it be started immediately. Half an hour later he was asleep after an intravenous injection of thirteen grains of amytal. He continued to be narcotized almost continuously. During these periods he talked a little in a drowsy way, still showing some manic tendencies. He required tube feeding.

Eleven days later the narcosis was terminated. In the drowsy state following this termination, the patient mixed up his words a good deal, became restless and was rather noisy the following night. The next morning however he was much quieter but somewhat confused and still unsteady. A week later, his condition having remained good, he left the hospital with his wife. There was a slight question as to whether he was not still slightly hypo-manic, but those who knew him said that he was no more so than he seemed many times when in his apparently normal condition. He was discharged recovered.

Diagnosis: Manic-Depressive Psychosis, Manic Type.

CHAPTER THREE

General View State Hospital, Westborough, Mass.

After driving for an hour, my father and the state troopers turned through the great stone gates leading to Westborough State Hospital, following a long, snow-banked driveway uphill. They arrived at the main administrative building, a vast red-brick Victorian bastion that formed the centerpiece of the Westborough complex. Founded in 1886, the hospital remained one of the largest psychiatric institutions in Massachusetts, housing somewhere in the region of two thousand patients.

At the time of my father's arrival, Westborough was run by Dr. Walter E. Lang, chief psychiatrist and superintendent, a man that my father neither liked nor respected. This being 1944, it must have been extraordinarily challenging to staff the hospital and to maintain basic standards during wartime, while so many men were overseas and with rationing still in effect.

My father had hoped to serve as a military doctor, but he was deemed ineligible due to his history of mental illness. Now, he found himself in the back of a police car, being transported to Westborough for his second stay in less than a year.

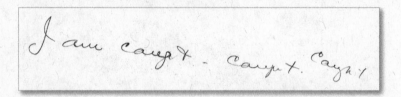

THE handcuffs were fitted tightly and were cutting into my wrists. They hurt a great deal. I did not complain but as I twisted my wrists and tried to make them more comfortable, the handcuffs seemed to close more and more tightly. I found out later that these handcuffs were actually equipped with a device that made them close more securely and tightly as the wearer struggles against them.

After admission, I was taken directly to a small cell in the upper floor of one of the violent wards. I sat on the edge of the bed. An officer had just released one of my wrists from its shackle and the key was still in the handcuffs. I toyed with these handcuffs as they dangled from my left wrist and, with the help of a few suggestions from one of the policemen, I loosened the steel shackle and handed it to him.

The state troopers went out the door, leaving three attendants with me. They directed me to remove my clothing. As I took off my garments, the reality of being back in a psychopathic hospital swept over me with added vigor. The damage of this procedure to one's dignity is inestimable. It takes away self-control; self-respect. As I took each article of my clothing off, I threw it to the attendants. My watch, residing in my vest pocket, took this aerial circuit, but was caught with the vest by an alert attendant and was saved from damage.

After the undressing procedure, there is always an embarrassing period while one stands naked in the presence of strangers. This embarrassment is relieved only in part by the drab clothing which is presented: ill-fitting white cotton underwear with long tight-fitting legs, ancient slippers and a ragged cotton bathrobe of fading color. Usually the underwear and robe are shrunken, and make one look too ridiculous. When one first sees oneself in the mirror after this change of clothing one might laugh heartily, if one had the courage and humor, but I was never able to appreciate the joke of looking so clownish.

Everyone left the room. The door was locked unceremoniously from the outside and I was alone. All was quiet. There wasn't much to see. I stood in a small rectangular room, measuring about fifteen feet long and ten feet wide by twelve feet high. There was a bed in the room, nothing more. The floor of my room was made up of a tile surface of a peculiar black and white design. A black line circled the middle of the wall on both sides. The wall was painted yellow above the line and brown below.

My thoughts dwelled for only a moment upon the nature of my surroundings. I was chiefly occupied with one intolerable fact: I was back at Westborough for probably a long stay. It would be many days before any word would reach me from the outside. I was in for the usual stupid psychiatric procedures—to go through once again what I had faced so many times before: an utterly meaningless period of confinement in a hospital under barbaric conditions inherited from a culture of darkness and ignorance. It seemed impossible that I could have been so stupid as to take any chances upon being caught in the same predicament which had seared my heart and soul so many times before, once again to have my mentality subjected to the destructive powers of loneliness, despair, idleness, filth, the ignorant dictates of below average doctors, lies and deception, the long absence from the strengthening power of work, isolation from all customary environment, disgrace.

I turned off my light and lay in bed. I fell asleep but awoke in a few hours refreshed. The door opened abruptly and three attendants entered the room.

"Come with us," one of them said.

I went along without argument or resistance of any type. Down the corridor we went, turning down a branch corridor at our right going towards the rear of the building. We passed through the shower room. There, bound fast in a straightjacket, was one of the demented patients whose nightly howling had disturbed me so much the year before. He looked pitiful and miserable as he pulled his head upward and forward to watch us pass through. Often he would jerk his head backward and forward in rhythmic sequence, his tousled blond hair, blue eyes and rounded, lumpy, scarred face made a sad and awesome picture; once encountered, never to be forgotten.

On we went into the next room where I was ordered to remove my clothing. I complied quietly. A straightjacket was brought forward and I was instructed to put my arms into sleeves that were built in a solid rectangular pattern. I was then told to lie on a bed standing at one end of an otherwise empty room, next to the window. I followed orders without making any comment, but with a mounting sense of indignation and deep despair. The straightjacket was made of canvas and strong canvas ribbons dangled from its edges in pairs. These were tied securely to each side and to the foot of the bed. The sixteen or eighteen such pairs of ribbons formed powerful anchors to the bed, allowing slight motion.

The attendants departed, leaving me alone with the light burning so that I could be watched through a large window from the adjoining tub room. I lay still for a while, trying to adjust myself to this new and most barbaric treatment. My dignity as a prominent practicing physician seemed to have been violated flagrantly. I felt insulted. A wave of despondency passed over me. I tried to imagine that the straightjacket was just a sort of mental test to be met by getting out of it as quickly as possible. I recalled some of the tricks I had read about in the life of Houdini. I remembered that he could untie knots with his toes and I began to practice. In a relatively short time, I learned a great deal about how to untie knots with a big toe and the first little toe of each foot. Slowly and methodically I went from knot to knot, untying all kinds of knots, and soon I was almost free.

Just as I was about to roll over and free myself entirely, three attendants entered and tied me down again, this time much more securely, leaving me little motion. Soon the attendants left, and—when they were out of sight—again I undertook to untie myself. It was a much more difficult task now that my motions were so limited.

In releasing oneself from an expert straightjacket, one can do little work until one has freed the ankles and re-moved the pillow that is fitted behind one's head. By making a heroic thrust of the head beyond a ninety-degree turn, one can just barely catch the cloth of the pillowslip in one's teeth. Having then caught the cloth, one can then pull and loosen the material enough to get a thicker bite and then, by raising the neck forward—simultaneously with thrusting the head to the opposite side—the pillow may be pulled out quickly. Then, more gradually, it may be shoved across the bed and down upon the floor. With the pillow removed, the head falls back to a lower level and the neck will descend through the opening of the jacket. It is then possible to move downward in the bed. The ankles can then be moved enough to make it possible to free them. As the feet move downward, there is a little play between the binding sheets and by rotating from side to side, and moving up and down, the feet come clear.

The next steps include loosening as many knots as one can reach after freeing the knees from the transverse binder. As one gets freedom of movement, some of the knots can be disposed of by putting the heel between the edge of the straightjacket and the iron rod to which the rib-bons are tied. A sharp downward thrust of the heel will then sever the attachment of the knot from its function with the jacket. Some of the knots around the top of the bed can be untied with teeth, but not always. Sometimes the arms can be freed from the jacket sleeve by flexing the elbows, which may then rip open the seams and allow one or both arms to be freed. If either of the top edges of the jacket can be loosened by teeth, hand or foot, the neck can then be removed from its noose by twisting and rotating it in a complicated series of movements similar to the progress of the head of a child as it goes down the birth canal. It will then be possible to climb out of the opening at the top of the jacket or at some section along the side. There are many ways to emerge, depending upon how the straightjacket is applied, and it is an interesting and absorbing study to work them out. Almost every new straightjacket application represents a new problem.

With patience and persistence, I soon had myself free. In came more attendants who fastened me to the bed with extreme diligence, using not only the canvas knots, but employing tight-fitting, heavy strips of sheeting across my chest, wrists and legs to limit motion even further. By a similar device my feet were strapped tightly together and then joined to the foot of the bed. Again I was left alone, and again I went to work, twisting and turning until I got my feet disentangled, then turning sideways and flexing my knees to get my legs above the rather powerful horizontal leg restraints. As I lay on one side, I was then able to work at untying the knots and could gradually loosen myself.

Time after time I wiggled free. The attendants returned at regular intervals to bind me down by methods growing more and more complicated and ingenious. They seemed surprisingly good-natured about all the trouble I was giving them. This strengthened my conviction that I was merely being put to some sort of mental test. One of them—apparently the one in charge—engaged me in a conversation about Schopen-hauer and various other philosophers as he assisted in the procedure of applying restraints.

As the night passed slowly, I grew to enjoy the task of escaping from restraints and gradually acquired the satis-fying conviction that I was doing about as well as Houdini himself might have done under similar circumstances (with no concealed files, scissors, or knives).

Dawn came. I had not slept. The night shift atten-dants—a fairly decent group of fellows—went off duty and the day shift arrived. Tiny Hayes, one of the physiothera-pists at the hospital, arrived along with a patient to take me to the toilet. Already my straightjacket was about free from its moorings due to my continued struggles. As my feet hit the cold cement floor, a wave of chilliness spread over me and with it, a wave of depression. Tiny and the patient, one on each side, guided me along to the toilet in the adjoining hydrotherapy room.

As I arrived at the toilet, Tiny caught a strap of my straightjacket and wheeled me around.

"Sit down," he said in a loud, superior voice.

I looked over one shoulder to get oriented, and then sat down upon a cold, unprotected, rather moist enamel toilet. The cold edge of the crude toilet seat seemed to cut into my flesh and it precluded any possibility of performing any functions.

"Hurry up!" Tiny yelled as he and the patient stood over me.

The situation was disgusting and humiliating. I arose with feelings of futility and walked back to the bed. A sense of anger seized control of me and, with a sudden twist of my body, I pulled myself almost free, but Tiny caught a portion of my straightjacket—which still held my arms imprisoned—and jerked me around, catching me from behind, closing his forearm over my throat, choking and hurting me. He dragged me to the bed and made me fall down upon it by twisting my neck. As he sat to buckle me down again, I caught his left arm with my right elbow. He turned and struck me a heavy and powerful blow with the flat of his hand on my left cheek. After this, he proceeded to tie me down with expert skill.

As soon as he left the room, I began to struggle to free myself. I could not tolerate these jackets. I could not restrain myself from resisting. When I was a patient at the Pennsylvania hospital, an attendant told me that he had watched me in restraints for a period of many days. He said that he had never seen me stop fighting restraints whether clearly conscious or narcotized.

After about two hours of struggling I got myself entirely free and stepped out naked on the bare cement floor, free from restraints for the first time in about twelve hours. I then grabbed hold of one of the steel frames used to drape curtains for screening off sections of the room. I was trying to use the frame as a bar to force my way through the steel window frame, when Mrs. Delaney, one of the day nurses, opened the door and walked in.

I was standing there, stark naked.

"Why, Dr. Baird!" she exclaimed.

"I'm sorry. I'm trying to cooperate but my body won't seem to let me yield to this type of therapy," I explained.

"I seem to fight restraints with automatic muscular efforts beyond my control."

She then closed the door and returned in a few minutes with underwear, bathrobe and slippers. I was then allowed to take a shower bath and put on these crude garments. I returned to my room and was locked in.

My memory remains quite clear for the events of the night and following morning. As I left the room where I was kept in restraints, lucidity of memory seems to persist, but as I stepped into the side corridor, a renewed sense of imprisonment came over me, and here my recollection of exact sequences fades. Things come back to me as vivid, indelible scenes that often return to be acted out again upon the stage of my mind.

Soon after reaching my room, a type of treatment known as "constant restraint" was put into effect. I do not recall having done anything violent or uncooperative, and the nurses on the ward told me later that I had given ideal cooperation. Yet for some reason, unknown to me then and unknown to me now, I was subjected to the most exhausting, the most painful and barbaric treatment which I can conceive of in this modern age.

CHAPTER FOUR

Westborough State Hospital, 1944

The patient was very excited. He was in an over-
talkative and overactive condition. He required
restraint, resisted with vigor, and with his
great strength, this was difficult. He destroyed
a great number of restraint sheets.

> I did so. Then began the
> agonizing experience of being
> wrapped tightly in cold sheets
> the initial

THE constant restraint procedure consisted in maintaining alternation between straightjackets and cold packs.

"Take off your clothes!" Tiny shouted.

I did so.

"Lie down on this bed!" he yelled again in a needlessly coarse and antagonistic voice.

I did so.

Then began the agonizing experience of being wrapped tightly in cold sheets soaked in ice water that were folded according to various patterns and laid across the bed over a rubber mattress. The initial impact of these ice-cold sheets on the spine is pure pain. Every additional contact with cold sheets as they are wrapped around the body brings chills and continued discomfort. First the arms are bound tightly to one's sides and then sheets are stretched in several layers across the shoulders, body, and legs, creating a trap that permits very little motion. Large safety pins are used here and there at strategic points to secure fixation. The process of wrapping Egyptian mummies must be similar. It's a rough business and the sense of complete immobility is uncomfortable bordering upon terrifying. Any normal individual would suffer from the feeling of being held so tightly. The manic patient—with his constant impulse toward over-activity of mind and body—suffers many times more than the normal individual might.

Restriction of motion is not the only source of pain. After the sheet wrapping and safety-pin-transfixing has been completed, transverse binders then bind one down further—across the chest, hips and legs. These are run across the body, beneath the steel bars at the sides of the bed, and back across the body, then pulled very tightly by the combined strength of two men, one working from each side. One attendant on the right, for example, will put his knee on your right shoulder and then holding the cross binder, will pull upward while pressing your shoulder down. The binder slips around the side bar of the bed and the sheet feels compressed. This attendant then holds the binder securely while the attendant across from him repeats the process. This is done by each of the attendants several times. The ends of the binders are placed across the chest and pressed down with enormous and powerful safety pins. The same procedure is repeated for hips and legs. Finally, one or two blankets and a sheet are placed over the wrapped body and a pillow under the head.

Everyone leaves the room. The door is locked. The shock of sudden coldness rakes the body with chills. Before long this deep sense of coldness begins to wear off and the body becomes heated. This heat quickly heats up the wet sheets, and the warm blankets prevent the escape of the heat. Soon, one feels hot and feverish. A great sense of restlessness comes over one.

From the beginning of each pack, the calf muscles feel uncomfortable, and no effort to change position will relieve this discomfort completely. Pulling the toes up, and then pushing them down, lessens the discomfort. One perspires profusely due to sheet insulation, retained body heat and violent physical exercise. As a result salt is lost and muscle cramps develop (as is well recognized in industries where workers labor in a hot atmosphere). In my own case, these cramps were noticed chiefly in the calf muscles, which were uncomfortable from the start. These cramps grow increasingly severe and become constant, agonizing.

While enclosed in a pack, the patient is required to pass his urine and feces into the pack—a diabolical ruling. I was always able to retain feces but I was forced to allow my bladder to empty after distention became painful. Once, when upset, my bladder sphincter seemed to go into spasm and, from the reclining position, I could not force it to open. Over a period of two or three hours, I suffered from increasing pain due to bladder distention. I begged and pleaded to be released so that I could empty my bladder, but I was merely told by Mrs. Delaney to pass the urine into the pack. It was explained to me that most patients derived pleasure from urinating while in packs.

It is difficult to get out of a pack, but possible to do so, and I have wriggled out of many of them. During the struggle to get out of the pack, the sense of being overheated is most uncomfortable. Heat builds up rapidly, due partly to the heavy insulation of the body, and partly to the violent exertion of struggling. Thirst becomes at first extreme, and then almost unbearable. Sometimes a nurse will bring water if one yells loudly enough, but usually one waits for what seems like an interminable period before water is brought.

After struggling in a pack from two to ten hours, one grows weak from loss of fluid and salt, from constant pains, from the disgusting feeling of lying in one's urine, from extreme thirst. The suffering is beyond the imagination of anyone who had not endured it. I feel sure that many times I found no sleep except in attacks of unconsciousness from which I would awaken probably in a few minutes. After these attacks of unconsciousness, I had the weird delusion of having slept for months or even years.

I can recall many occasions when I would suddenly break into a cold sweat and great drops of perspiration would pour out upon my forehead, nose and cheeks and run in rivers down across my face and neck. I believe that these phases of sudden, extreme, cold-perspiration and these attacks of unconsciousness represent dangerously severe stages of exhaustion.

After many hours, I was always so weak that I could

hardly raise myself from the bed. Sometimes an attendant placed his hand behind my head and raised me to a sitting position. When I then tried to stand, I usually found that my leg muscles were so cramped, and the rest of my muscles so weak, that I could not stand up. While being taken to the bathroom, I walked along stooped over, half crawling, with my knees bent and attendants holding me up. The next privilege was to sit on the toilet, sometime clean, and sometime smeared with urine and feces. As soon as I had finished at the toilet, and washed my face and hands, I was returned and placed immediately in a straightjacket without being allowed any period to recover from weakness, cramps, exhaustion and disgust. With the straightjacket came another type of suffering to succeed the one just endured.

For several successive days and nights this torture was continued. My body and mind fought on savagely and ceaselessly, but automatically. In spite of extreme sensations of exhaustion, I found no sleep, except in brief spells of what I believe was unconsciousness. I was never allowed any food except while under restraint. Usually Mrs. Delaney or Mr. Burns fed me—occasionally Tiny Hayes. Mr. Burns was more considerate in the feeding procedure than either Mrs. Delaney or Tiny Hayes. Tiny was usually brutal; Mrs. Delaney only a little less so. Breakfast was just a bowl of thin hot cereal without cream or sugar but with a little milk. A tablespoonful of this gruel mixture came at one's mouth before the previous mouthful could be swallowed. If one did not open and swallow what was offered quickly enough the stuff would usually be emptied partly around the mouth, and it would run in disgusting little rivers down the cheeks onto the neck, finding its way into pack or jacket.

Once, after Tiny had fed me two or three spoonfuls of breakfast cereal, my mouth was so full that I couldn't accept any more and I turned my head to one side as the next spoonful came toward me.

"Don't you want your breakfast?" Tiny asked in his usual booming, insulting voice.

"Oh don't bother about feeding me!" I replied, even though I was hungry.

"That's all we need to know," said Tiny and left the room, taking my breakfast.

He did not return.

Once when Mrs. Delaney was feeding me my Sunday dinner, she fed me so fast that I could neither enjoy the food nor swallow it fast enough. I began to vomit.

Thus on many occasions, hunger was added to thirst and cramps, the pain of loneliness and incarceration, the agony of restraints, and the sudden details of torture which a staff of state hospital psychiatrists can devise.

AFTER some several days of this torment, Tiny Hayes, Mr. Burns, a powerful attendant, and a patient came in my room. They freed me from the bed and, leaving the straightjacket still on me, they took me—partly dragged me—to the bathroom. I felt particularly brittle, perhaps even filled with hatred. When I was brought back, the straightjacket was removed, and there was a pack already laid for me.

I backed into a corner.

"It seems to me that I've had enough of this sort of thing," I said.

A wave of resentment swept over me. I clenched my fists and decided to fight rather than endure this agony any longer. Quickly, I turned toward the group and, with my blood boiling in anger and my eyes betraying the sudden change of temper, I advanced in a swift powerful movement of aggression. All four men turned pale and fell back. They showed surprise and real fear. Without striking a blow, the moral victory was mine.

I let my hands drop.

"All right, I'll go through with another pack," I said.

The four men came back cautiously as I lay down on the cold wet sheets. Two of them lined up on my left with Tiny Hayes at my right shoulder and Mr. Burns next to him near my feet. My head was raised off the bed. Suddenly I saw a long black rounded object coming down toward my head. My astonishment was so great that I made no attempt to duck away, though I was free to do so. I remained motionless as the instrument struck me on the right side of the forehead. The blow was painful. As the black object returned to Mr. Burns' corner it looked as if it were bent in the middle. At first I thought it was a piece of lead pipe, but later I learned that Mr. Burns used a piece of heavy rubber hose on the patients and carried it in his pocket. The blow that he delivered to my forehead produced in its right upper portion an area of soreness with excoriation and swelling. A large vein in this area was damaged and went into a state of varicosity, protruding conspicuously. The soreness lasted for two to three weeks and the excoriation for almost a month. After eight months, the vein has begun to return to its normal proportions. The staff psychiatrist, Dr. Boyd, examined the area but said nothing.

ON Sunday, two or three weeks after my admission to Westborough, at around 10 a.m. it was announced to me that visitors were on their way over. I lay there in my pack: cold, hungry, tired, weak. After a wait of ten minutes or so, I heard footsteps in the hallway and, through the gap in the partly opened door, I could see Gretta and our family physician, Dr. Porter, walking along together. They came into the room and greeted me. Gretta kissed me. We talked. Both Dr. Porter and Gretta kept on their winter coats. The room was frigid. The ground outside was covered with snow. A cold wind was blowing.

"Do you want a divorce?" Gretta asked.

This question struck me as a very serious one to put to a person supposedly ill. It came at a particularly difficult time. I thought for a few seconds.

"Yes," I said.

Dr. Porter then immediately made some remark about how to obtain the divorce and the expediency of employing "cruel and abusive treatment" as a basis for the procedure. The conversation ran on about this and that.

I began to talk about the barbarities of the treatments I had been given.

"Well, Gretta, I guess we'd better go," Dr. Porter said.

This remark gave me an even stronger feeling of having

to battle all alone, with no help to be expected from friends or relatives.

Dr. Porter asked whether I wanted him to leave the room so I could talk with Gretta alone. At first I asked him not to leave and then, in a little while, I requested that he leave us alone for a few minutes. Obligingly he left the room and stood outside talking with Mr. Burns.

"I'll miss you a lot!" I told Gretta.

My eyes filled with tears that fell in copious amounts and rolled down my cheeks. Gretta began to cry, too, and as she leaned forward to kiss me, her tears fell upon my eyelids and cheeks.

After we had been alone together only a few minutes, Dr. Porter returned. He seemed upset to observe us both weeping. He and Gretta hurriedly said goodbye, and they departed. The total visit was a short one.

At dinnertime, I was extremely hungry but also lonely, blue, discouraged, cold, and tired. A full tray of food was brought in and laid on a table near me. It was a fairly good Sunday meal with chicken that actually had an appetizing aroma. The attendant then left and was gone for about three quarters of an hour. This trick of leaving my Sunday meal there to grow cold—while arousing my appetite and neglecting to feed me—I supposed was part of my punishment. Before the end of an hour, however, the attendant returned and fed me. I made no complaint.

During the remainder of the day I lay in the pack quietly without moving, only as necessary to relieve in part the agony of calf muscle cramps. I lay there, still as death, never calling for water nor making any requests at all. I made no attempt to get out of the pack. It seemed wise to yield quietly to the treatment. At about seven in the evening, I was released from the pack but transferred immediately to a straightjacket. I said nothing. I cooperated to the best of my ability.

CHAPTER FIVE

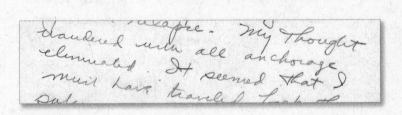

THESE days of constant restraint were the darkest of my life. I cannot imagine exploring greater depths of discouragement and hopelessness. I knew then—and I know now—that I became delirious in a way previously unknown in the course of any of my illnesses. These spells of delirium were brought on by the harsh treatments employed. I am sure of this.

During the hours of my flights from reality, I passed through phases quite foreign to anything I have ever experienced before. As I lay there bound down, I lost all sense of time and season and imagined that scores of hundreds of years were passing by. I imagined that some strange power of eternal life had been bestowed upon me and radiated to those who came within my immediate encasement. From day to day, nurses and attendants seemed to grow younger. I felt sure, however, that my friends and relatives on the outside were long ago dead and that I would never see them again.

My thoughts wandered with all anchorage eliminated. It seemed that I must have traveled back through subconscious impressions imposed by every stage of the evolutionary tree. My dreams and thoughts focused upon the origin of man, the nature of his soul and the nature of eternal life. I visualized the migration of a tiger-like creature that flew on silver wings from a distant planet to earth, thousands of years ago. This imaginary creature was interpreted as a forerunner of man, and looked like a saber-toothed tiger, with a coat and wings of silver. I could see these creatures stalking prey, their tongues out-stretched in hunger and rage. The tigers struck down smaller animals and ate entire carcasses, sucking blood, voraciously.

In my dreams I could see the saber-toothed tigers as they took to upright positions, a force of gravity slowly changing the shape of their heads and other parts of their bodies, developing into savage, primitive men. These men rode large, powerful, and very fleet horses with hair growing to great lengths. These riders of that ancient age used no saddle or bridle but buried their legs and hands into their horses' long hair, and each man seemed to become a part of the horse he rode. The hair, which was twelve to eighteen inches long, was very fine and quite translucent, and carried a magnetic field. The lines of the field radiated in all directions, covering a space many yards beyond the dimensions of the horse. It seemed that these magnetic waves were transversed by the rays of the sun and that the horses were able to travel along beams of sunshine like a railroad on its track. I could see these horses and their riders migrating by the thousands to and from earth, and going off vast distances from the earth, visiting Mars and other portions of the universe. These dreams were so vivid that I believed they were a true reflection of some primitive state of the earth, leaving behind recollections in the vast subterranean passages of the human mind to which one could find access in certain mental states.

I dreamed about the soul and discovered that it was a magnetic field, partly shaped like a human body, but with dimensions far greater. It seemed that nobody could have life without these magnetic fields of which there were only so many available. As the child took shape in its mother's womb, such a soul would migrate into it. Other souls would wander off to seek a new type of existence on some far away planet. Conceived in this way, the soul and eternal life seemed comprehensible qualities, and understandable. Such a soul living on forever could see and hear and think, but could not be seen or heard. On the basis of this conception, it is easy to explain why the souls of departed ones do not come back and appear to us. In my dreams, these souls came back and sought out loved ones, but could not make themselves seen or felt. However, this did not make them unhappy and thus free from all earthly lives, they soared away to play among sunbeams and moonbeams and wander eternally through the universe, finding constant companions. Others chose to live life again and found their way into newborn babies. I found much happiness and reassurance in these dreams about the soul and eternity.

My thoughts dwelled upon world affairs: the war and peace and how to deal with Russia and Japan and Germany. I must have talked constantly about the ceaseless flow of ideas concerning these enemies. I pictured a peace conference which would deal in a Christian manner with both Germany and Japan, allowing these countries to choose their own leaders, subjecting them to no humiliation, no poverty, to ensure peace by some far-reaching educational system and not by force of arms alone. There is no way to know whether the development of the science of destruction will make it possible for human beings to destroy each other completely, but it does not require much use of imagination to visualize the horrors of the wars to come, robot bombs lending greatly to this vision of the future.

I talked out loud at nighttime, alone in my room, about these thoughts, dreamed about the use of Christian propaganda to help win the war, perhaps employing skywriting to replace leaflets as a means of reaching the common man in Germany and Japan and later Russia. I visualized a near future date when skywriting could be done in flashing colors at night, with music, thunder, and other sound effects.

DURING the next several days I lay constantly in restraints, never moving, never making any requests, cooperating silently. Some of the patients came to my window and tried to tease me into getting out of restraints. I took no notice of this and made no reply, kept my eyes closed, lay still, slept very little. After three or four days the restraints were gradually used less and less and finally discontinued. A table and chair were brought into my room. I entered a slightly more normal way of being. My secretary sent several boxes of sharpened pencils and some paper. A small amount of additional paper was obtainable at the hospital. I began to write this story and to describe my experiences, my dreams, my thoughts.

Then, one Friday, three or four weeks after my admission to Westborough, I was told that visitors were coming to see me. Immediately I went to the bathroom to wash my face in cold water, collect myself, and comb my hair. I was still dressed in my sackcloth and ashes hospital underwear to my ankles, slippers, and a drab bathrobe. As I darted into the bathroom, I could see coming down the hall Gretta and Dr. Means, my friend and former faculty advisor at Harvard Medical School. They were waiting for me when I came back to my room. Greetings all around were warm and friendly. I kissed Gretta and we sat down to talk. I was in good shape, only mildly manic, but I had just drunk a cup of coffee and this made me very talkative. I read them letters that I had written and then gave them to Gretta to mail. I talked too much.

Gretta seemed upset that they would not give me my own clothes.

"The whole plan of treatment has been brutal in the extreme, but I don't mind it," I told them. "I write complaints to my lawyer, because I think it's the logical thing to do—but I really don't mind it at all."

Gretta wept a little.

"He's such a good sport about it all," she said.

Passing comments were made about the divorce. We talked on at length. I related the chain of events leading up to my manic depression cycles—going back to the high points of the original development of the attacks.

I could see tears in Dr. Means' eyes.

Mr. Burns, the attendant, came to the door and I introduced him.

"You're cooling off all right," Dr. Means told me. "Your chief problem is to stay on the right side of Dr. Boyd. He's your chief critic at present."

Dr. Boyd was my appointed psychiatrist at Westborough. Later I spoke of the harsh treatments I had received, saying, "I think that Dr. Boyd should be put through these treatments so that he'll know what he's doing when he prescribes them in this way."

"That's logical," said Dr. Means.

The total visit wasn't long.

As I walked down the hall with Gretta and Dr. Means, I slipped my arm around Gretta's shoulders and she slipped her arm around my waist. When we got to the nurse's office, Dr. Means stepped aside to tell a joke to Mr. Burns. As Gretta and I stood there she seemed like such a child, and her arm around my waist seemed so small and so delicate.

I turned to her and said, "I'll always want you to be at my parties and to help me."

She looked at me and smiled. Dr. Means shook hands and went out the door first.

As Gretta went through the door she stopped and we kissed. The tears were streaming down her cheeks and, as I came away from her, I could see great sorrow in her face. Mr. Burns said that she cried all the way downstairs.

After the visit by Gretta and Dr. Means, no one came to see me for about six weeks. During this time Saturdays and Sundays seemed especially long because they were days when so many patients had visitors. Often on Sundays a nurse or an attendant would say, "Dr. Baird, you will surely have visitors today." I soon learned that when this remark was made, no visitors ever came. On days when visitors did come, I usually learned of it because someone said, "You will have visitors in a few minutes. They are on the way over."

Perhaps Gretta didn't come to see me because it upset her to do so. Perhaps other people didn't come because the hospital authorities wouldn't let them. The effect of having no visitors was agonizing. No greater loneliness or despair can be imagined.

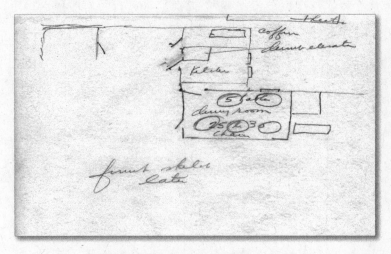

Perry's sketch of the ward at Westborough.

CHAPTER SIX

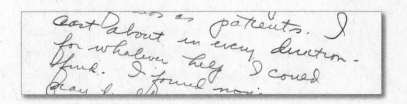

AS soon as I was beyond the period of restraints I began to write a great many letters to friends and relatives. A hospital ruling allowed only two letters per week. I got around this by enclosing many letters in my one letter to Gretta, and by requesting that she forward them. Though she had never done so previously, Gretta began to forward practically all of my letters.

I wrote several letters to my friends among Boston physicians and described the conditions at Westborough. None of these physicians seemed to show either interest or sympathy.

One wrote: "The sooner you start cooperating with the Westborough authorities, the sooner we'll be seeing you again."

Another wrote that the abusive treatment I received from attendants was probably due to my own attitude towards them.

Several times I wrote to Bob Fleming, the new psychiatrist who had taken over my case when my former psychiatrist, Dr. Tillotson, gave it up. Since I had been unceremoniously dumped into a cell at Westborough, I had had no communication from Bob. I wrote him several times. I received no reply. I wrote asking that he give up my case unless he was willing to do something to help me out. I wrote my lawyer and asked him to consult other friends of mine among Boston psychiatrists, and see if one of them would take over. I also wrote directly to the following psychiatrists: Dr. Donald J. Macpherson and Dr. Colket Carver. Colket wrote me, "I'd rather be your friend than your psychiatrist."

My lawyer consulted with Dr. Donald Macpherson about several matters. Donald promised to come out to see me—and did so at the end of eight or nine weeks. I wrote to a close friend, Paul Chandler, and asked him to come to see me. He wrote and said that he would, but he never did. I wrote Dr. Ben Ragle and asked him if he'd take over my care. He replied that he made it a rule not to accept close friends as patients.

I cast about in every direction for whatever help I could find. I found none.

I pray to God that in the future I shall be able to remember that once one has crossed the line from the normal walks of life into a psychopathic hospital, one is separated from friends and relatives by walls thicker than stone; walls of prejudice and superstition. It may be hoped that psychopathic hospitals will someday become a refuge for the mentally ill, and a place where they may hope to recover through channels of wise and gentle care. But the modern psychopathic hospitals I have known are direct descendants of ancient jails like Bedlam, and I believe that they do harm, not good. The brutalities that one encounters in state and city psychopathic hospitals must be the by-product of the fear and superstition with which mentally ill patients are regarded. For the present, the best one can hope to do is to stay out of these places, pity those confined there, and to do what one can to accelerate the slow process of mental hospital reorganization.

With several friends, my secretary, Gretta, and a few relatives, the correspondence was regular and strenuous. The almost daily arrival of one to a half dozen letters brought me a great deal of comfort. Possibly this correspondence created a wider spread of gossip concerning my illness, and it may have done me a bit of harm in various ways, but it was a gratifying experience at the time of the illness, and it did much to reestablish normality.

DURING perhaps my seventh week at Westborough, Corny Trowbridge—our Chestnut Hill minister—paid me a visit. I did not expect him and I don't know why he came, but I shall never forget his visit. Naturally we talked about spiritual values. I told him that bible teachings had been much impressed on me in childhood days. He spoke of Christ.

"Surrender to Him," Corny told me. "It isn't as weak as it sounds. Surrender to Him."

Corny went on to say that by following closely the teachings and the example of Christ, one could realize so much more in the line of success and happiness.

"Christ lived these 1,944 years ago," I said. "There must be some spiritual viewpoint more adapted to our modern age. In place of surrendering completely to Him, might there not be some way of just going along with Him, beside Him?"

I spoke of my marital troubles and my hunger for a satisfactory sexual life. I narrated my love for dogs, horses, and birds at some length. I gave Corny two letters about some difficult bareback riding I'd done. I explained that my deep love of horses enabled me to understand them better and to do with them things that most people could not accomplish.

As I talked about my love of animals, Corny was reminded of St. Francis.

"St. Francis must have been a manic depressive," he said. "Have you ever heard about his sermon to the birds?"

He went on, telling me the historic account of St. Francis and the birds he loved.

"Haven't you read *The Life of St. Francis*?" he asked.

"No," I replied.

"I shall send you the book if you'd like to read it."

As Corny and I talked, I believe pleasantly, he let me have some of his cigarettes. We both smoked. It came time for him to leave and I walked with him from my room to the visitor's waiting room where he had his hat and coat. As he picked up his hat and coat, I could see that his eyes were moist and his voice betrayed emotional tension. He said that he'd come again to see me. I wrote him several times asking him to come and wrote my wife several times to ask her to request that he visit me again. He never returned.

Soon after Corny's visit, a book entitled *In the Steps of St. Francis* arrived in the mail. It was the story of St. Francis's life blended with a description of travels through Italy and other countries where he had wandered with his followers. As judged by a card I found in the book, it must have been a Christmas present to Corny from some relative. I read it through the first time, rather haltingly, because I did not enjoy the travelogue part, but later as I reached the end, I was so deeply interested that I immediately went back to the beginning and read the entire book over again, consuming in detail all the description of the author's travels in the steps of St. Francis. As I went along, I underscored passages and made marginal notes. It was my intention to send Corny a new copy of the book, and I wrote asking my wife to arrange this for me. She never did so and eventually she returned to Corny his own copy, somewhat worn from much use and considerably altered by underscoring and marginal notes in pencil.

FROM my window looking out over the hills in back of the hospital there were small illuminated crosses that could be seen near the tuberculosis unit and also in the woods to my right and occasionally on a hilltop. During the daytime, on this same hilltop, I could see three objects sitting in a row. I could never make out exactly what they were. They corresponded closely with the location of crosses seen at night and sometimes flashes of light came from them. These flashes of light were quite baffling, as were the crosses. I never really understood how these crosses happened to appear. Other patients could see them, and one was visible from the porch to the right of the women's active wards in an easterly direction.

Someone told me—perhaps a patient—that some women from Chestnut Hill were living in nearby dormitories.

For a day or two, I fell into the delusion that they were women I knew. One night, I lay with my head in the ventilator shaft in my room and talked, thinking my voice might reach a particular woman I imagined might be in an adjoining dormitory. I quickly lost these amorous impressions.

I couldn't seem to prevent myself from performing pranks. I loved to hide forks and spoons inside the large metal sleeve through which the ceiling light hung down. This bronze-colored, conical sleeve was broad at its base next to the ceiling and could be unscrewed and lowered, leaving a fairly large space. Quite a good many small objects could be put in here, and the sleeve could then be put back in place. When my spoons and forks disappeared, the attendants searched my room but could never find them until I revealed the secret. All this seems childish in retrospect, but at the time it seemed to relieve monotony. I felt that my wits were pitted against those of doctors, nurses, and attendants, and I loved to tease them in many ways. The large safety pins, used to help bind the patients in cold packs, could be concealed in the electric light fixture or could be hidden by hooking them on an iron pipe concealed about a foot up the ventilation shaft. Through a small hole in the mattress, small articles could also be concealed.

I made many attempts to find ways of unlocking my door, usually with crude keys made from bedsprings or by using sound vibration produced by hammering on the doorknob. I also tried the scheme of hooking the iron crossbar at the foot of the bed over the doorknob, then manipulating the bed to produce various types of torsion, stress and strain. One day, I succeeded in breaking the steel rod connecting the inside and outside knob. Another day I took the inside knob off and hid it in my left upper jaw. As I did so, Tiny Hayes came suddenly into the room.

"Where is the doorknob, Perry?" he asked.

I took the doorknob out of my mouth and handed it to him.

TO ease the pain of incarceration, I sang and whistled many tunes day and night: "Rose Marie," "Desert Song," "Indian Love Call," "Intermezzo," and many others.

While whistling and singing at night, I stood in my window and tapped in rhythm on the panes. One night, as I was tapping on the windowpanes leading to the porch (quite gently it seemed), one of the panes suddenly broke. It wasn't at all like the break that comes after a powerful direct blow, where big pieces of broken glass are produced. It was more like physical forces together with sound were creating the effects, shattering the glass into thousands of small pieces. On the same evening, a pane of glass in the window with outside views broke in the same manner, and under the same circumstance. I recall going to great pains to help attendants pick up every tiniest piece of glass.

For many days during this time, the light bulb held my interest. I never knew what type of bulb it was, but it seemed to contain a gas, perhaps a mercury vapor, which took on a kidney shape when the light was turned on. As I found my eyes persistently upon this bulb, the kidney-shaped vapor would slowly change with other shapes, round and oval, and sometimes it looked like false teeth, opening and closing slowly as in laughter or conversation.

Westborough State Hospital, 1944

The patient became very destructive, completely destroyed several iron hospital beds, broke the panels from the door of his room, broke the sashes from the window, dismantled the window casing and with a window weight in each hand was very threatening toward the employees but did not strike them.

CHAPTER SEVEN

DURING the course of my time at Westborough, I became convinced that many patients entered Westborough in a state of mild mental illness but were made critically ill, or even hopelessly ill, by the procedures employed and the rough handling by nurses and attendants. The doctors play an inconsequential part. There are so many patients that it is impossible to give adequate attention to any patient. Everything is run on a crude, general plan. The keynote of the place is incarceration. Movies are available to the convalescent patients twice weekly during certain months of the year and small groups meet together to sing and dance. A small orchestra made up of patients functions periodically. There is a department of occupational therapy. But so far as I could see during my stay, these sources of distraction formed an insignificant part of the care of the patient. Perhaps before the war—and before there arose such a difficult problem of funding adequate trained nurses, attendants and occupational therapists—the whole set up might have been quite different. What I saw with my own eyes during a trying wartime period was ghastly.

There were many patients who came and went and many

who were with me from start to finish. Old Mr. Sullivan, who drooled at the mouth, sat in his filthy clothes and smoked a corncob pipe. He was mostly rather quiet but sometimes cried out as others pushed him around. He didn't like to be shaven so would avoid shaves if possible. It wasn't difficult to figure out why. Being blind, he had to rely upon Tiny Hayes to shave him. I witnessed one such shave. Tiny delivered the shave while an assortment of nurses and attendants held Old Mr. Sullivan down. He groaned and cried out in pain. His head was jerked around quite roughly and held in strained and uncomfortable positions while Tiny scraped with brutal violence, leaving the skin red and excoriated.

Mr. Sullivan was a frequent companion to Mr. Clark, also senile and mischievous. They often sat on the bench outside my window, talking and growling, Mr. Sullivan smoking and drooling from the mouth and Mr. Clark performing constant pranks. One day I saw Mr. Clark blow a red balloon out of his right nostril like a clown in a circus. Where he got the balloon and how he learned to blow it, I do not know. He and Sullivan often wrestled on the concrete floor, foolishly and clumsily. It afforded much amusement to many of the patients. I could never get much kick out of the exhibition, however.

The age range of patients was from about eight years old to eighty. There were two youngsters, one very young and attractive, around eight, and the other about ten or eleven. They were both profane and mischievous. These youngsters wrestled on the concrete floor and amused us in many ways. One of them, the redhead, made it a specialty to steal up to my window and spit in my face. One day I called him to my window and threw a glass of cold water in his face. This was the only revenge I took, except to spank him and give him a little gentle jiu-jitsu.

One day the attractive Italian lad, Angelo Cephalo, whom I had met the year before, arrived on our ward. I was in the office as he was brought in to surrender his clothing and go through the usual routine. I observed that he seemed about the same except that his shoes, in contrast to last year, were quite shapely and stylish. They were small and fit him well, whereas the preceding year, he had worn large shoes that gave his feet a whole appearance of bourgeois effect. He was now good looking from head to foot, neatly built and well proportioned, very athletic. When I was allowed out of my room, we competed in every respect: wrestling, boxing with open hands, tumbling. I got the best of him in every competition.

One of my special tricks was climbing the steel posts on the porch. I could jump from the floor, grasp the steel post with one hand and knee, and climb like a monkey, quickly touching the ceiling and sliding quickly back down. I could do this easily while manic but with great difficulty while normal. Another patient, Clare Johnson, would be the coach in some of our competitions. He'd give the signal and we would both leap to a steel pole (there were two of them). I could usually touch the ceiling before Angelo had left the floor. We did it again and again. Both Angelo and Clare seemed amused at the speed with which I could get to the ceiling.

Peter F. Perry was the most colorful character on the ward. He had been a favorite patient of mine when he was working regularly and had a little money. I treated him for syphilis. I remember doing a spinal fluid exam and finding it normal. Evidently he developed central nervous system syphilis of the paretic type and was sent to Grafton State Hospital, another psychiatric institution. After seeing him at Westborough, I could recall his letters from Grafton. He owed me some money and could not pay. He had asked me to wait. He never admitted he was at the hospital in Grafton. I had finally cancelled his debt, never knowing why he couldn't pay.

Pedro was a nice-looking, middle-aged man, a Portuguese. He had handsome well-chiseled features and a full head of hair. His skin was swarthy, his figure trim and powerful. Evidently he had boxed professionally and wrestled. His hands were exceptionally powerful. He could bend steel bars with his teeth. After extracting a steel bar from a bed, he would wrap a piece of cloth around it, put it between his teeth and pull on each end with his hand, bending the bar slowly, to a sharp angle. I tried the trick. With my limited experience, I could make no progress. Pedro also had his own shorthand, a peculiar variety of the Morse code, and he had mathematical tricks for adding and otherwise dealing with large sets of figures. His voice was fairly good, he sang fairly well. One night I heard him give an informal oration on the porch. His elocution was surprisingly effective. Every morning he would be kept quiet in a straightjacket or tub bath and before lunch he would be released. He then would take a shower, if he'd been in a straightjacket, and dress. He came regularly to the porch, singing and tap dancing for us, often dancing with some other patients. He seemed to sleep very little. Pedro usually spent every night, most all nights, in the bathroom, writing and smoking and composing music, and probably living in some dreamlike imaginary world.

Agnes was a nice-looking redheaded girl, living across the court. She often sat in the window. We exchanged a few letters by way of an attendant. She wrote me a poem or two. Someone said she was a manic depressive at only nine-teen, and had been at Westborough for ten years. When I finally met her at close range, I found that although she was dressed in a very youthful garment, her face with its lines betrayed an age of thirty or more. I have often won-dered who she really was. One day in the auditorium, where we had music, singing and dancing in small groups, I was dancing with her on the stage. There were only a few others around. She coaxed me into singing "Rose Marie." I sang a few bars, felt greatly embarrassed, and quit.

There was a man with a badly mangled hand. He had only a finger and thumb left on each hand. He was a middle-aged blond, very good looking, friendly, evidently paranoid; a patient who'll be here a year or two. He'd been an engi-neer, seemed very sick when one tried to talk with him at any length, but for a brief conversation, was quite rational. He had told me that his hobby was constructing various types of engines. We talked about engines, drew diagrams and then tried to figure out a new and more efficient die-sel motor. He developed a contact dermatitis of the front of the neck. This was treated in a rather unorthodox manner, and became abscessed. He had to go to the surgical ward for incision and drainage. Frequently his wife, son, sister and other relatives came to see him. He sat for long hours talking with them. He had a work assignment somewhere in the place. I never knew just what he did. I considered him a good friend.

There was a dark-complexioned young Italian, thin and delicate, black hair, deep brown eyes, and small of stature. Once I shook his hand and found his palm hot and moist. He ate very little and what he did eat, he ate hurriedly, getting in and out of the dining room very quickly. He sat all day, in a corner alone, or at the window, talking to himself quite constantly. Perhaps he was conversing with some imaginary person. I never saw him speak with any other patient. No one ever paid any attention to him. He seemed to be beneath notice by any of the doctors. He was a pitiful figure. I imagined that he would go on for years, talking to himself, too poor to afford expensive therapy of the "total push" type. Perhaps "shock therapy" will reach Westborough someday and pull him out.

One patient, a tall, good-looking blond, about twenty-five years of age, came up to see me a few times when I was extremely manic. We talked at great length. We played an imaginary game of chess, using a drawing of a chessboard, and relying upon our memory of the plays. He conceded me the game.

"That's the easiest game I've ever won," I commented.

Later we played a real game of chess on a real checkerboard with good chess pieces. He defeated me in the one game we played.

On the ward was a pitiful old man, of average height and trim, his hair silvery gray, his eyes blue. He always stood by himself in some corner away from the rest of us, dressed in underwear and a white bathrobe. He talked incessantly, repeating some monotonous succession of words, over and over again, literally for hours without end.

"Oh God, oh God, oh God," he would say.

Or, "Take it easy, Mister. Take it easy, Mister. Take it easy, Mister."

Obviously he was lonely, in great distress, but he talked rapidly and in a tone that had astonishing powers of annoyance. I never saw him have a visitor. He aroused my deepest sympathies, but, after weeks of hearing his loud and rasping murmurings, I too could understand why so many patients could not endure his, "Oh, God, what'll I do? What'll I do? What'll I do," by the hour. Often the poor old fellow would be put in a straightjacket and placed in a room by himself, behind closed doors, to shut out his voice. Almost daily, patients and attendants would drag him out of his corner, throw him on the bed, scold him and even beat him. He always showed fresh bruises and scratches. One morning his right ear was greatly swollen with subcutaneous hemorrhage, a typical boxer ear injury; the kind that frequently goes on to a cauliflower ear. Evidently someone struck him a vicious blow on the ear. So far as I could determine, the staff never paid any attention to the poor old man's injuries, and they made no attempt to stop the beatings that he received.

A young man, about thirty-eight, with soft, delicate skin and a heavy beard, spent some days with me on the violent ward. He never said much, but often he would look at me and remark: "What's the story?" (pronounced "storree"). I used to show him how I could whistle to the robins and get them to hop up to the window on the south exposure of the porch. Several did what they could for me. Sometimes I whistled and brought robins up in pairs. They would hop around until they got near the porch, and then, as I continued to whistle, they would fly straight up into the air, heart-to-heart and beak-to-beak, in a mating flight. Soon after this, the young man was discharged and left the hospital.

After about a month, my behavior had become exemplary in all respects. I said little and confined my activities to eating, sleeping, walking in the corridors when permitted, washing the corridor floor, dignified conversation with nurses and attendants, and courtesy to everyone.

Up to this time, I had seen nothing of the hospital superintendent, Dr. Lang, but as favorable reports filtered through to him, he came over to pay me a visit.

"All manics are the same," Dr. Lang explained. "There was no use in my coming over until you had improved . . ."

In other words, when I got sick he turned me over to his assistants and stayed away from me, but when I was well, he delegated himself as my physician and advisor.

"It occurred to me that you had been treated too gently by your psychiatrist friends in the past," Dr. Lang went on to say. "When you were admitted this time, I gave directions for you to be treated just like anybody else."

"Well, they sure laid it on heavy," I replied. "I would never have believed that psychiatric care could be so rough."

Dr. Lang's manner tended to indicate that he was pleased with my rapid recovery and thought that treatments had made this recovery possible. I wanted to tell him my recovery was in spite of these barbaric methods, not because of them, and that I believed that the brutal treatments had much to do with the unfavorable course of my illness. As the course of events proved, my illness became the longest and most disastrous in the history of my case. Dr. Lang's ignorance, his old age, his total lack of any humanitarian viewpoint totaled up to the most unfortunate influences that have ever come into my life. I am sure that he has wrecked many lives that might have been salvaged.

"I shall try to cooperate with you and Dr. Boyd during my present stay with you," I said to Dr. Lang.

"We don't expect you to make any promises."

"Well, anyway, I'll play ball with you."

"That's all we ask. Perhaps you may not agree with my views but maybe we can work together anyway."

After his thirty-minute visit, Dr. Lang got ready to leave.

"Thank you very much for coming to see me," I said. "I'm glad to have had a chance to know you. Your visit has been very pleasant."

After another week or ten days, comments were made to me to the effect that I might be transferred downstairs, out of the violent ward.

Mr. Burns took me down. Before we left he said, "Look out for Mrs. La Point downstairs. She may cause you some trouble."

MRS. La Point was a small, broad, strong-looking woman with dark skin, deep brown eyes, graying black hair and large protruding teeth which flashed as she talked and stood out prominently when she laughed. She was need-lessly matter-of-fact and cold in her reception. Her voice was loud, coarse and capable of rising into a high-pitched resonant quality. She herself was nervous and irritable, easily angered and often spontaneously angry without evident cause.

When Mr. Burns introduced me, Mrs. La Point ignored this formality.

"Your box will go into the hall closet," she said, "and when you need anything we'll unlock the door for you. I'll assign you a bed later. You may now go on the porch."

As I stepped up on the porch, I stopped and looked about me. Here was a collection of about thirty patients sitting around in chairs, ranging in age from six to sixty. Few patients seemed to be looking at me, but the dead silence suggested that everyone was completely aware of the event of a newcomer. I went around and greeted the patients whom I recognized, chiefly those who had been with me upstairs and had moved down ahead of me. Among them were Angelo Cephalo and Clare Johnson.

The porch was essentially a recreation room furnished with four tables, four benches, straight chairs and rocking chairs, and a pool table. The floor was cement. Large sliding windows with glass panes began at the waistline and rose almost to the ceiling, providing an almost-solid glass enclosure to permit an excellent three-sided view of the hospital grounds and distant fields and hills.

Soon after, I sat down to get my bearings and to read some letters. Some of the younger patients came and suggested games. I played with them then, and on succeeding days: bridge, poker, checkers, and after six p.m., pool.

I'll never know exactly how it happened, but one or

more patients were constantly intruding upon my thoughts and actions. Many of them acted very strangely. One man, gray-haired and intelligent, about fifty years old, played checkers a great deal with me. He played well. When I defeated him, he wept openly, not loudly, but with tears streaming down his cheeks. The way he wept upset me. It didn't seem that losing the game made him weep. It seemed that he wept because I was so greedy and cruel in beating him so badly.

I HAD asked my secretary to send over some photographs taken while I was riding in various horse shows. One afternoon, they arrived in the mail. The patients showed a great interest in the pictures and asked for copies. I let them have the pictures on request. Sometimes I brought out my box of letters to read some of them again, seeking comfort.

"He's brought out his box again," one or more patients would say.

I couldn't understand why my box annoyed them.

We were allowed to bathe once weekly and to shave every other day. The bathing involved either shower or tub and included no unpleasant feature except standing in line and doing one's ablutions in the presence of six or eight other patients waiting their turns. The shaving involved the same old unpleasantness of using equipment just used by a succession of preceding patients. The toilet seats were less dirty than upstairs, but frequently showed stains of urine and feces. Every night we all went to bed at 10 p.m. and were awakened at 5:30 a.m.

"Time to get up!" an attendant would shout.

There were two dormitories containing ten beds each, and a third containing about twelve. One room contained four beds. It was my debatable privilege to sleep in the four-bed room with a disgusting looking fellow with a hare-lip and a throat healing from a slash inflicted in a suicide attempt. Another roommate was a well-educated young man who talked intelligently about chemistry, but very insanely about astronomy. His chief disadvantage as a roommate was that he snored loudly and constantly, all night long. The third companion in this room was a former patient on parole. He slept during the day and worked nights as a supervisor on another ward.

The food was unsavory and monotonous. On all wards, it was the same: a bowl of hot cereal with one glass of milk, but not cream or sugar at breakfast. The only way I could eat the cereal was to lay on some butter and let it melt, mixing it with cereal, adding sugar and eating with Courage. Extra milk was usually available as well as cold bread and butter. Coffee was always served in large tin pitchers from where it was poured into heavy porcelain cups. Luncheon and supper were colorless meals, often malodorous. The vegetables were cooked dry without seasoning. Meats included hot dogs, meat loaf, fish and salt pork. The salt pork usually had an odor of putrefaction. Milk and bread. Hot black tea without sugar. Desserts: Jello, pudding, and so forth. Every Saturday night: beans with a little pork fat. Milk and bread, no butter. Tea without cream or sugar. Several times at lunch they served a most delicious honeycombed tripe, but I can recall very few meals that were eaten without, proverbially speaking, the fingers holding the nose.

I did more than my share of the daily work. Every morning before breakfast, I swept the porch floor and collected the dirt in dustpans from which it was transferred to large trashcans. I swabbed the floor with a mop and moved the furniture, first to one side of the room, and then to the other, to permit a thorough mopping job. Usually I had a great deal of help for these procedures, but sometimes I did most of it alone. During the day, I was active in keeping all trays empty and I helped sweep and mop the corridors. Often in the evening I played pool with Clare Johnson, Angelo Cephalo, the man who wept when I beat him at checkers, and others. I played pool with skill that astonished me, and somehow executed shots that I never expected to succeed.

The radio blared out constantly: music, boy detective stories, news broadcasts, and so forth. From 5:30 a.m. until

10 p.m. I was subjected to this wholesale barrage. I felt the pressure of great strain. It was difficult to sleep until everyone else went to bed, and hard to sleep then on account of snoring. Sometimes at noon I was so tired that I could hardly stand on my feet. I would occasionally sit and lean my head on my arms, but it was against the rule to lie down until after supper around 5 or 6 p.m. when the room and dormitory doors were unlocked. My cheeks became hot and red.

One bright morning, I pulled a table over beside a bench and sat down to write a letter. Mrs. La Point rushed onto the porch.

"Put that table back where it belongs!" she yelled.

At other times, Mrs. La Point would suddenly appear on the porch, and seeing a patient lying on a bench would shout, "Get off that bench!"

Her crude manner must have upset many of the patients.

Mrs. La Point succeeded in putting me under a great deal of strain and she contributed to my strange relapse: the most extraordinary adventure I've ever had in the realm of the unknown frontiers of human existence.

CHAPTER EIGHT

Westborough State Hospital, 1944

The patient quieted down to a considerable extent, and was transferred to a quieter ward, but his over-activity increased and a week later he again became so overactive that it was necessary to retransfer him to a disturbed ward. During the manic stage at times he was quite confused and was boastful, extravagant in his statements concerning his physical strength and financial success. He wrote voluminously but a large part of his production was disconnected and exhibited an exaggerated flight of ideas.

> *my friends & relatives on the outside were long ago dead & that I would never see them*

I GREW nervous, sensitive, weak, sleepless. I recall walking alone in the corridors of the hospital and living over again in strangely vivid daydreams. My life seemed extremely important to the world—poor fellow that I was, locked up in a state institution, pitied and looked down upon by so many, headed for many grave personal disasters. I imagined that our ward was at the center of the world's attention. In some way I concluded that we were all in a building as transparent as glass, and that for a mile up into the sky and all around were stands accommodating hundreds of thousands of people (or perhaps souls, because I could not actually see that which I imagined.)

The events of my past life took on new meaning. I could see myself as a hero in every fiction tale I'd ever read: *Count of Monte Cristo, Three Musketeers,* and so many others. Suddenly I was Houdini, The Count, and a hundred other legendary characters. I grew more and more ill in a world overgrown with delusions.

I spent much time watching the birds, robins, grackles, and sparrows playing around on the grass and in the trees. One day, an attendant came out of one of the buildings and threw some bread out for the birds. I imagined that my own love for the birds had influenced the gesture. I whistled for the birds, talking to them in their language. They were always easily coaxed to the place near where I stood to whistle to them. I had many delusions but no hallucinations: I saw and heard only what was actually there.

Mr. Burns came walking down from the administration building. I imagined a crescendo of laughter and applause from the unseen and unheard galleries above me. I watched him closely as he strode along across the grass. He walked all the way around the three walls of the porch and climbed the fire-escape stairs to the upper floor. I followed him along, talking to him and teasing him. He looked larger than usual, his face broader, whiter. His fat, white uniformed body seemed to have increased enormously in size.

Mr. Burns said, "Would you like to go back upstairs for a while?"

A delusion took hold: perhaps they were closing the upstairs on account of some impending catastrophe, and maybe they wanted me to go back to be sure that my own room was about as I left it for future historians to study.

I went with Mr. Burns; we walked upstairs. The soles of my feet were becoming so sensitive that I could hardly stand on them. I moved along slowly and quietly, down the corridor to my room. Mr. Burns stayed behind. There were no patients anywhere. I went into the closet and rearranged the slippers, towels and bathrobe, putting everything neatly in order. I went into my room and looked around. I laid one end of a towel on the window and closed it, leaving the towel hanging down. I took down the shade and rolled it up, thinking of it as sensitized photograph paper that held some type of record. I put this beneath the mattress, running it beneath some of the links in the steel bedsprings, thus fastening it down. I rearranged the bed clothing and turned to leave the room. An attendant came and locked me in. I was deeply shocked. I sat down.

A little while later, I was let out and wandered around, finding that all the patients had reappeared. Perception of color became more intense. The lips of most of the patients looked intensely red, unnaturally so, as if they had on a coating of very dark lipstick. I walked around saying nothing, doing nothing, bewildered. An attendant came and took me to my room. I was placed in a straightjacket: The shock to my sensibilities was profound and painful. This straightjacket was new; fresh canvas made specially to fit me. It would have been extremely difficult to get out of it. I made no attempt. What bothered me was not the mechanical excellence of the straightjacket and the difficulty of getting out of it, but the utterly incomprehensible puzzle of why I was put in it when I was doing nothing but cooperating to the best of my ability, fully and completely.

The hall clock must have stopped running, or if it didn't I was no longer able to hear its ticking. Everywhere there seemed to be a ghastly silence. On the porch I could see many patients familiar to me, but I could not hear them talking or walking. They were all moving around incessantly but soundlessly. My north window was partly open, but no fresh air came through, and I heard no sounds from the road below.

My imagination took on the speed of light. I thought that the entire Westborough region had in some way become detached from the Earth and was catapulting through space like a rocket ship. Either a movie camera left running had produced the ghostly figures on the porch, or else these poor patients were trapped with me. The silence continued.

I lost all sense of time. I knew that Earth was hundreds or millions of miles away. I felt sure that several hundred years had passed and that if I ever got back to Earth all the people I had known would be dead and gone. I whistled "Intermezzo" and talked aloud to myself. The chart of my travels through space seemed to be toward Mars and I feared I might get stranded there. It occurred to me that other planets might be pleasant places to live, but I wanted to get back to Earth, even if all the people I knew were dead. It occurred to me that thought-waves were the only influence that I could exert to get the ship back to Earth. I sang and whistled and talked, trying to find the combination. Days, weeks and years rolled on by. No one came in my room. No one brought me food. To test reality, I made my bed jump up and down, and I made it move around and around the room.

Once, as I was making my bed jump up and down, I heard a crashing of boards and the bed seemed suddenly to get jammed in the floor and I couldn't move it. This made me imagine that the hospital building had been placed on wooden boards on a lake and that I had created a vibration with my bed that had crushed the boards and let the building sink to the bottom of the lake. For a while I thought we were at the bottom of the ocean between Greenland and the British Isles.

After what seemed an eternity I heard voices in the hall and some attendants came in and gave me food. And then I was left again to silence, loneliness, to roam lost in the universe. Night came and lasted a hundred years. In the morning the attendants came and took me to the bathroom. I sat on the toilet quickly, then climbed over the partition into the toilet next to the window. I seemed unable to speak. I clutched the window tightly, looking at the glorious morning sun. The attendants had to drag me out by force.

Another morning came. I detected an odor of exhaust gas coming through the window as I lay there in my straight-jacket. I surmised that everyone in New England except us had been killed by gas released by the Japs. I dreamed of thousands of Japs disguised as American citizens invading the Boston area, and I dreamed of an earthquake that made the Ritz Hotel topple over. My heart and soul were rent in agony.

While I was trapped in this delirium, my wife and secretary came in with the sheriff to serve the divorce papers on me. My secretary was to serve as witness. I remember nothing of the episode, but my secretary related the facts about as follows:

She and Gretta entered the room first. I was lying on the bed. The attendant came in and said I had visitors. I rose and sat up in bed. Eleanor, my secretary, put out her hand. I did not seem to see her hand or her. I did not shake hands. I rolled over toward the east window with my back to my visitors.

"Dear, if you don't feel well we'll come again some other day," Gretta said.

Eleanor identified me as Perry Baird. The sheriff served his papers.

Gretta wept all the way home.

ONE day Mr. Burns came in with several attendants. I was loosened from my moorings to the bed and allowed to get up. Wandering around my room, perhaps a little confused, I recalled the night when I was tapping on the windowpanes and two of them became shattered into small pieces as if broken by sound vibrations. I stepped up to the north window and brought my right fist down against one of the small panes of glass. The blow was much too strong and the glass broke with large sharp fragments with dagger-like

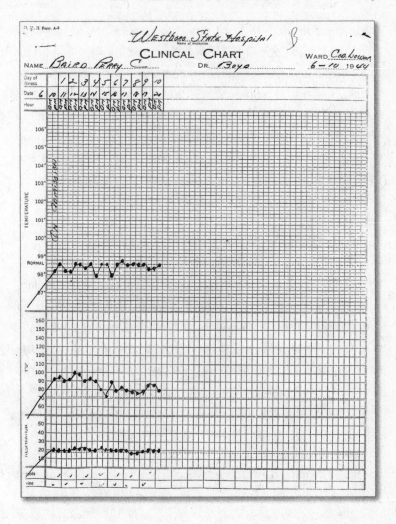

edges. The top of my right hand near the inside of the wrist was deeply cut. It bled profusely through an opening a little less than an inch long and evidently extending through the full thickness of the skin. There was a smaller puncture wound over the sensitive flexor surface of the wrist on its wide portion next to the bone. Blood also poured lavishly from this small opening. Many drops had been splashed on windowpanes untouched by my fist and the floor was mildly stained. After a rather long interval, several attendants collected outside my door and came in together, expecting trouble. The night supervisor bandaged my wrist. Healing took place rapidly at the site of the larger laceration but seemed slow in reference to the puncture wound. Several times, without any injury or other provocation, the puncture wound began to bleed spontaneously and required a compression bandage.

This strange, dreaming state may have lasted for only a few days. The thought delusions were realistic, convincing, horrible, but they gradually passed away. It would be impossible to recall all details of these agonizing days.

One night I woke up and found myself in bed, the straightjacket gone. Two letters were there. Attendants came in and asked me if I wanted a shower or a bath. I took my letters with me, holding them as I took my shower. They were ruined by the soap and water. After the shower, I began to feel better and I managed, in a matter of a week or so, to make a rapid recovery from this strange mental state.

When I first began to walk, the soles of my feet were so sensitive that I could hardly bear to stand up on them. Peter F. Perry was around most of the time to let me lean on him, my arm around his neck. I would tiptoe along in this way and gradually gained confidence, losing that extreme generalized hyperesthesia.

Easter had come and gone. I made more and more

friends among the patients. I thought about God, Christ and many spiritual values, as I had never done before. I recall seeing four airplanes flying across the sky, in the shape of a cross. I felt close to God, but did not feel happy. I wondered whether God would give me some special job to do, whether my sufferings might come to have some meaning, lead to some spiritual goal, some great destiny.

MY next visitor came in the evening: Captain Charles I. Johnson of the U.S. Navy. I was never so glad to see anyone, as I was to see my very good friend, Charlie Johnson. I shook hands with him at once. I shook hands with him again. We sat and talked continuously for two hours or more. Charlie questioned me about the history of my case and he delved into possible precipitating factors: marital unhappiness, disappointment over not being in the service, and so forth. After our long talk he said, "I think we're getting somewhere now."

As he left, Charlie promised to see Dr. Harry Solomon, chief psychiatrist at Baldpate, a private hospital, to try to arrange my transfer to there. I knew Charlie would do everything possible to help.

CHAPTER NINE

LATE one afternoon about ten days after his first visit, Charlie Johnson returned, bringing Harry Solomon with him. Charlie was hoping to persuade Harry to permit my transfer to Baldpate hospital.

"Would you be willing to go to your family in Texas for a year after your illness is over?" Charlie asked.

"Yes but I'd like to think that my own vote about such a step would be reckoned among the others," I replied.

Charlie then said: "During your illness, you have the reputation of being a pathologic liar."

The words fell hard upon my ears. I have a passion for truthfulness and I will never tell a lie if there is any way of evading the question, ignoring the question provoking the lie, or if there would be any way of checking up. I recognize that, about once a year, one may get into a difficult situation wherein something of the nature of a lie may be the best way out—and a thoroughly justifiable way out—but I pride myself upon being able to deal with such situations without deviating from the actual truth. It is true that I may tell a "tall story" once in a while, building up a good adventure tale around some unusual personal experience. Each such story, however, always has considerable basis of fact, and the added color is for the sake of humor, or for the sake of making a good story. I have done this twice in the course of the last three years, and never before in my life. I shall always wonder why Charlie said what he did. I believe that one of the foremost essentials to the development of power and clearness in thinking lies in the habit of telling the truth, knowing the truth, believing the truth, and thinking the truth. Any person yielding to lies and deception as the easy roads out of tough situations will usually get in the habit of careless thinking in general, and they will suffer the penalty of losing a keen intuition in regard to probability and improbability, truth and falsehood and even right and wrong.

Dr. Solomon said several things of special interest to me.

"The manic does not know what he is doing," Dr. Solomon said.

These words from Dr. Solomon taught me that even a man of his distinction, experience and education could fail to understand the manic. I can only say that, in my own case, my memories are quite clear of events taking place during the manic state. All of the things which I have done have been with the full consciousness of what I was doing and why I was doing such a thing. The quickness and impulsiveness of action and speech, however, can have a very disquieting effect upon others, and it is hard to maintain good judgment and full awareness of the effect of one's actions upon others. But one is not in darkness and one is fully conscious of all that is going on. The only limitation on memory is that so many things may happen in such rapid succession as to impair recollection of details.

Sometimes, however, I wish Dr. Solomon were correct and that one really didn't know what one was doing. Then one's consciousness would not hold one responsible for what one had done, and all memory of events taking place during the manic state would vanish. Then one could return to the normal walks of life, like an alcoholic who couldn't remember anything he did while drunk. One could probably negotiate a return to normality with less probability of going through a depression. After returning to normal health, however, it is inevitable that the events of the preceding manic state will crowd back into consciousness and harass one. The feelings of self-criticism, shame, and embarrassment are true foes and they can become so violent as to inflict the deepest wounds, undermining self-confidence and making it hard to face the world. Unfortunately, Dr. Solomon, you do not understand the manic psychosis. I wish that your words were true. I wish that one could forget, or that one didn't know what he was doing, that one had nothing to remember.

This led me to wonder whether a doctor who had been manic once or more times might not have insight better equipping him to understand and treat the manic. But where is such a man to be found? It would require the combination of going through the illness, and making a complete and perfectly lasting recovery. In my own case, it would require making a far better recovery than has been manifest in the last few years and it would require changing over to the field of psychiatry. This would involve a great financial loss and other adjustments that might be most difficult.

After a rather long talk with Dr. Solomon, he seemed to

conclude that I was mildly depressed. As I stood there, he came forward and put both hands affectionately upon my shoulders and shook me a little as if to try to impart some degree of Courage. After this I took Charlie and Dr. Solomon to my room and showed them the adjoining porch. Dr. Solomon recognized an old patient on the porch and went out to speak with him.

As he did so, Charlie turned to me.

"You have sold yourself to Dr. Solomon," he said. "I believe he will take you."

BY now, I was quite well again, calm and quiet. I had regained poise and showed no symptoms. The day came for me to go downstairs again. Before going downstairs, I knew what was in store for me: I knew that I must endure again all the same sources of fatigue, stress, strain, and indignities. As I came down to the lower ward and entered the nurses' office, Mrs. La Point greeted me as before, roughly and coldly. I spoke to her as cordially as possible. After putting my things in the hall closet, I moved on down the corridor and went into the bathroom to comb my hair.

Angelo Cephalo followed me and tried to make me read a letter he'd just received. I declined to do so.

"I'm not interested, thank you," I told him.

I said this not just to be discourteous but because Angelo had contributed to a portion of the strain that had caused my setback. He had said strange things to me that I tried to comprehend but couldn't. He would walk up to me and look at me intently, with a facial expression of mixed anger and annoyance.

"I haven't my whole life to stay around this place," he'd say.

He seemed to imply that his stay at Westborough had something to do with my stay there and that it was up to me to get us all out.

I knew before I arrived again on the lower ward that Angelo, Mrs. La Point and many others would be powerful sources of distress to me. I was determined to resist all influences tending to upset me. I left Angelo in the bathroom and went out onto the porch to say "hello" to some old friends.

During the days that followed, I learned how to maintain spiritual equanimity in spite of an atmosphere of constant irritation. Angelo did his best, following me around and complaining loudly and unpleasantly about the food, hospital conditions, and so forth. Once at dinnertime, Angelo was sitting across from me, protesting about the food and making unsavory remarks. I exploded, clutching the knife at the side of my plate, and rising from my seat in anger. Then I quickly settled back and ate my meal in silence. I had made some very caustic remarks. I cannot exactly remember what they were.

One old man, a wealthy Italian, sat at the breakfast table one morning and ate his cereal with loud slop-ish sounds, making many unnecessary and disgusting noises. My reaction to this was to make similar gustatory noises while drinking my milk. This same old man had a way of sitting in a chair and passing intestinal gas with loud reverberations, all very unnecessary. He had a horrible face, only one or two dirty teeth remaining, a large, frequently protruding tongue, brown eyes, thick head, heavy beard, large bony frame, clothes filthy, but hands finely shaped, soft and delicate as a woman's. He never said much, laughed boisterously, showing his teeth and filling one with mild feelings of disgust. He was a weird but unpleasant-looking character. His hands however seemed to indicate fine birth and talent.

The radio broke down and was taken away for repairs. It never came back.

I played pool a little but found that, now that I was normal, my game was very poor.

Except for two or three outbursts, I kept my peace, moving away from Angelo when he came around, staying alone most of the time, maintaining a policy of friendliness, but tending carefully to my own business and staying out of other people's affairs. I walked the corridors at frequent intervals and took an active part every morning in sweeping and mopping the floors, emptying ashtrays, and so forth. I read many books: *The Robe, Grapes of Wrath, West with the Night.* I read *In the Steps of St. Francis* again, devoured the daily newspapers *Herald* and *Traveler,* and enjoyed my daily mail. I wrote fewer and fewer letters. I came to the realization that, in spite of the fact that my correspondence meant so much to me, my letter writing was being held against me. I reduced my letter writing to the barest minimum, and, when I did this, I received more privileges very quickly.

During the days when I was reading *The Robe,* Mrs. La Point would come every day to the porch.

"Dr. Baird, come and get your robe!" she cried out. A

great deal of this teasing and hazing went on constantly. My bathrobe, slippers and pajamas were kept in a locker room that was only opened as necessary for a patient to get what he needed. At the end of each day, the room was opened so that all of us could get what we needed for the night. I don't know why Mrs. La Point so often came and made that loud announcement, "Dr Baird, come and get your robe!"

During my return sojourn on the lower ward, I was assigned to a ten-bed dormitory and slept second from the window. One day, a Negro appeared on the ward. It so happens that this Negro was assigned to a bed opposite mine in the dormitory. I knew that being thrown in company with him would not bother me. He was a quiet, well-educated Negro with a light-chocolate color. During the first few days he always seemed to stay at a distance from me as he wandered around on the recreation porch. Gradually I made his acquaintance. We talked about poetry and religion. He read my book *In the Steps of St. Francis.*

Clare Johnson sat in the toilet for hours every day and worked with a file and a knife handle, making a key for the door. One morning he had a strong odor of liquor on his breath. I have often wondered where he got the liquor.

The gray-haired middle-aged man who had always wept when I beat him at checkers was still on the lower ward when I came back there. Soon after my arrival, I walked up to him.

"Would you like to play a game of checkers?" I asked. "Do you suppose you could play without weeping?"

We played several games; he wept no more.

———

ABOUT ten weeks from the date of admission, after ten weeks of constant confinement, I was allowed to go outside with a group of other patients to enjoy the fresh air, walking and basking in the sunshine.

My first day out was an occasion to walk ceaselessly in a circle of concrete walks in front of the auditorium. Dr. Boyd came along and watched me a moment.

"It's the greatest thing in the world," he said.

"What is?" I asked.

"The open air," he stated.

One afternoon, after walking a great deal alone and with Dick Condon, I sat for a few minutes on the auditorium steps to listen to the orchestra play some pieces I liked. This orchestra was composed of a pianist, a drummer, and a violinist. They did very well together. Miss Francis, a nurse and Director of Entertainment, as well as occupational therapist, came out and asked permission of the attendant to bring me in. I was coaxed to play the piano and did play a few pieces I remembered. The members of the orchestra praised me, perhaps excessively, but they made me feel a touch of happiness.

MY private psychiatrist, Bob Fleming, came out to see me, bringing with him my brown Palm Beach suit. As he walked along slowly in the morning sunshine, all his clothing—from hat to shoes—was dark and grayish in color, rather drab. He was a little stooped as usual, and he cast about himself a somber, lugubrious shadow. His face was dark, his eyes dark, his features expressionless. He looked strongly Northern, taciturn, fathomless, like some wicked perpetrator of an evil plot. My heart did not beat in gladness as I saw him coming. He had never answered any of my letters.

It was his third visit in eleven weeks. He sat and talked, seemed very nervous, acted as if he'd rehearsed his speech and faltered here and there, as if he'd forgotten some of his lines.

I began describing to him the extreme torment of treatments by means of straightjackets and packs.

"The only way I could tolerate these measures was by working out a game to get out of them as quickly as possible," I said.

"They were a relief, weren't they?" Bob asked, as if to imply that these harsh and brutal methods had relieved some nervous tension.

I made no answer to this comment. It proved to me how little insight into the barbarities of state hospital methods could be exhibited by anyone who hasn't been through them.

"I'd like to see you go back to your practice," he remarked. "When you're on the job, you are one of the best-adjusted doctors in Boston. Dr. Lang won't let you leave now, but we can get you transferred to Baldpate. He can't prevent that. Once we get you to Baldpate, I believe we can get you back to your practice very soon."

"How long will it take to arrange the transfer?" I asked.

"Only a few days."

This conversation took place in my room.

"You can bet your bottom dollar that every word we said was overheard," I said as we walked out.

"How do you know?" asked Bob in an obviously nervous pitch.

"Oh, in various ways," I replied. "I have opened the door several times unexpectedly and found patients and attendants standing around and listening. This has only been when I had visitors."

EARLY one afternoon soon after Bob's visit, the attendant came to my room.

"I don't know whether it's good or bad news," he said, "but you are to be transferred to Baldpate in an hour or two."

It was six weeks after Charlie Johnson and Harry Solomon had come to me and said they'd arrange it in ten days. A suitcase was brought over and I packed my things. Later an attendant took me to the office where I obtained my watch, wallet, driver's license, draft card and a check made out to Baldpate for the $97 I had.

Dr. Rickless came by.

"Are you really going to write that book?" he asked.

"Why, yes, certainly," I replied.

"Well, be as easy on us as you can," he commented as he went through the door.

"Goodbye," I said softly.

Outside a limousine was waiting with a driver and one assistant. We drove away. After about ninety-five days at

Westborough, ninety-five days of mingling pain, discomfort, suffering, loneliness, ninety-five days that I shall never fully understand, it was a relief to sit there in a comfortable limousine, a pleasure in itself just to move along the Worcester Turnpike and rest my eyes on the countryside with its vastness and its springtime loveliness after being confined for such a long time.

It was a pretty day. As we drove through Chestnut Hill, I wanted to ask the driver to stop at my house so that I could see my children, but I did not make the request. I felt sure it would be against the rules and I did not want to ask special favors. We drove through Boston to the Newburyport Turnpike, and on to Baldpate.

I said to myself: When I get to Baldpate, I shall meet a new group of people: doctors, nurses, attendants, male and female patients. I know that I shall encounter things that may upset me. I shall remain calm. I shall cooperate. I shall make no attempt to escape. I shall prove that I have made a complete recovery.

CHAPTER TEN

B aldpate was a small private sanitarium located in Georgetown, Massachusetts, about two hours' drive from Westborough. Once a popular inn, the main building—a Victorian
clapboard with gables and porches—sat on a small hill, over-
looking a lake and farmland. At the time of my father's arrival,
the sanitarium had only recently been established under the
guidance of a gentle Austrian psychiatrist named Dr. George
Schlomer. (Dr. Schlomer became a favorite doctor of the poet
Robert Lowell, who stayed here in the 1960s.) Baldpate was
known as one of the more progressive institutions in Massachusetts. Dr. Schlomer believed that patients should be given their
freedom within hospital grounds, and patients were allowed
to go to the lake and even into the nearby town, as long as
they obtained permission. In order to stay there, my father was

required to prove he was peaceful enough to enjoy Baldpate's many privileges. The understanding was that if he became too disturbed or violent, he would be moved elsewhere.

The day of his arrival, a psychiatrist named Dr. Buck Rose came out to welcome my father. Dr. Rose had treated my father in the past and knew his case well. He wrote the following notes in the Baldpate records:

Baldpate Hospital, 1944

On admission, Dr. Baird seemed tense and somewhat restless being anxious to talk but in particular reference to his experiences at the State Hospital during the past 95 days. During his time at Westborough, he was threatening, restive and extremely destructive, destroying several iron hospital beds and various other parts of the hospital structure. Four months later, however, he seemed much quieter. He was admitted to room 19 where he was served his supper. After supper he fitted in well with the routine of the hospital and entered in social activities at the house.

When seen this morning he stated that he had a comfortable night without medication and has an entirely different feeling about life. He is confident that we will find him completely normal and will be willing to discharge him soon. He states that he wishes to cooperate in every way and promises repeatedly that we will not be sorry that we have taken him and that he will cause no trouble.

I have personally known this man, both as a friend and as a fellow physician, for eight to

ten years and it has fallen to my lot to have seen
him in several of his psychiatric episodes. On
several occasions I saw him at the Boston Psychopathic Hospital and on one occasion at the McLean
Hospital. It is of interest to me that I saw him
in December at the Harvard Club and anticipated
at that time a manic break, warned him of it, and
suggested that he see his private psychiatrist,
Dr. Fleming. As I talked with him today, I am
impressed with two things:

1. He is not as depressed as I had expected.

2. He is suggestively hypo-manic and is a
little flighty in his conversation and manner.

Knowing the patient, I wonder if he is not in
a period in which he is able to control himself at
times, but distinctly not well. I do not antici-
pate any serious trouble however.

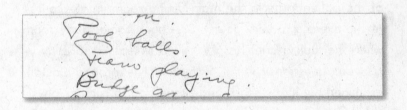

AFTER being greeted by Dr. Rose and unpacking, I sat by
the window for a while, and then walked around to see the
grounds and to enjoy the feeling of having a little greater
freedom. At about 4:30 p.m. I was sitting in a chair beneath
a tall, majestic tree. As I looked down through the woods, I
saw a section of Baldpate Lake glistening in the afternoon
sun. I heard footsteps on the grass and stood up as a doctor came forward and introduced me to the hostess; young,

blond and attractive. He left us together and we talked and walked along. Suddenly she had the inspiration to drive me into Georgetown so that we could pick up her Victrola and records for dancing that evening. The doctor gave his permission for me to go along. The trip was not a long one but it breathed of added freedom. The blood coursed more gladly in my veins.

We returned to the hospital and played some records. I met a great many patients. They must have been about twenty-two in the main building, another group of ten or twelve confined to the more active unit.

Soon after my arrival an attractive, blond youngster came up to me.

"You are our guest," she said. "We are happy to have you here."

That first night, I had supper alone in my room. The rest of the patients ate in the main dining room. In the course of the evening, a very Jewish Dr. Cohen came to my room where he took a brief history, asked several apparently irrelevant questions about dermatologists around Boston, examined my many scars and carried out a cursory physical examination. After he had finished his investigations, he looked at me.

"You are as completely normal as anyone I've ever met," he said. He paused before adding: "But your record is bad."

Dr. Cohen went on his way. I stayed in my room a little while and then joined the other patients for dancing. The first evening passed on by with faint memories of dancing, pool, and bridge. I remember leading a group of youngsters in a few songs. Though I was entirely inexperienced at this sort of thing, I got through the job fairly well. I danced with several of the women patients and had a good time.

I shall never forget any of the patients I met that night, though I do not recall their names: a very attractive woman from Houston, Texas; a girl of twenty-one from Texas; two physicians; Harry, of M.I.T., mustache, athletic, highly intelligent; several elderly women; Emma; a young woman divorced, from France; Betty Winn.

At 10 p.m. we all went to bed. A nurse knocked at my room and asked me whether I needed sedatives or hot milk for sleep. I had no such need. I slept well.

The attractive youngster who had greeted me upon my arrival came to me the next day.

"You were wonderful last night, Doctor," she said. "You are a great man."

FOR the next ten days, life was easier for me. There was more diversion and more recreation, more freedom. Here and there were flower gardens, hedges, a tennis court, a barn converted into a recreation and occupational therapy unit, an old-fashioned swing and facilities for croquet. I enjoyed the almost daily trips to the auditorium. Several times there was bowling, participated in by several mixed teams selected from both male and female wards. Trips to the canteen—to buy candy, ice cream, Coca Cola, cigarettes and newspapers—provided brief periods of relaxation.

Having been schooled at Westborough to rise every morning at 5:30 a.m., I awoke automatically at this hour, or earlier. The other patients were not usually awake until 7:30

a.m. I made a special effort to be quiet, sometimes stayed in my room and read, or walked around the grounds. There was an attractive divorcee who sometimes woke early and joined me in my early walks. The very first morning, she took me to the basement and showed me a mother cat and her kittens.

Each morning, except Sunday, was spent in the occupational therapy unit, a remodeled part of the barn. Here were available the usual activities: weaving, sewing, carpentry, etc. There was a piano and a book of sheet music very familiar to me: *Piano Pieces the Whole World Plays.* The occupational therapist was blond and middle-aged—a high-strung and quick-tempered but attractive woman. We played the piano in duet a great many times.

One morning, I was sitting at the piano alone, thumbing through the pages and playing all the easy pieces as I came to them. Perhaps a little thoughtlessly, I came upon "Home Sweet Home" and played it. The Houston, Texas woman, of whom I was very fond, raised her voice in protest.

"Don't you know better than to play pieces like that when you are in the presence of people who are depressed?" she asked.

"I'm so sorry," I said. "The comment which you just made interests me a great deal. I'd like to talk to you about it sometime."

"You're only a dermatologist!" she retorted, sarcastically.

I made no reply to this, but went on playing a few pieces and then quietly slipped out the door, wandering over to the main building. I wanted to be alone. I walked into the large front room where the patients played pool and ping-pong and danced.

I stood there for a few minutes, and then into the room walked the attractive Houston woman who had made the cutting remark about my being "only a dermatologist." Apparently she had followed me over.

"Do you want to play some ping-pong?" she asked.

"Surely," I replied.

We played for a half hour or so and then several of us went swimming.

ONE beautiful morning a large crowd of us went to the lake to have lunch there and spend the afternoon. It had been implied to me that I would be expected to read a new book, *The White Cliffs of Dover.*

Soon after we had finished a lunch of hot dogs and coffee, we all sat down beneath some shade trees and the therapist in charge handed me that lovely book, *The White Cliffs of Dover.*

"We'd like to have you read this to us," she said.

I took the book.

"If anybody would like to do the reading in my place," I said, "I'd be delighted to arrange it."

"I'm making all the arrangements around here," said the therapist, that quick-tempered, blond woman. Most of the patients stayed around to hear the reading, but some strolled down to the lake beach to bask in the sunshine. After the reading of this story of the glory of England there were a few compliments and in the next two or three hours others drifted in.

I sat talking with the therapist and two or three patients at the ledge above the road going down to the beach. We talked about St. Francis. I spoke of how he gave up all his worldly goods. The therapist raised her voice in disagreement with so insane a gesture.

"Whether you agree with his teaching or not, here was a man of courage," I pointed out. "Can you imagine having the spiritual fortitude to do as he did? He tried an experiment: he tried to follow exactly the teachings of Christ and he followed them as best he could, living out the full length of his life by his teachings."

A pause in the conversation followed, I arose and wandered down to the beach and went into the water, swimming around. Miss Emma was out in a rowboat, having trouble. I swam over and caught hold of her boat, towed her back to the shore.

"Lady in distress!" I cried.

Emma and I reached the opposite shore. She played around in the water.

"Let's go into the woods," she said. "I'm curious about you."

Emma was not good-looking, but she did have an alluring figure.

"You go into the woods at this point," I replied. "I'll swim down a little ways and go in there. I'll find you later."

I swam down the lake. Emma obligingly followed. I walked into the woods. Emma followed me. I lay down in the grass. Emma lay near me. I couldn't make love to her. She was a patient at Baldpate. She wasn't good-looking. She wasn't alluring.

Emma and I left the woods after a short stay and swam back across the lake. The afternoon grew long. In a lengthy, bedraggled line, in twos and threes, we wandered back along the road. Dr. Rose passed in his car. He didn't offer to pick us up.

After my walk in the woods with Emma, I made some joking remarks about the episode in the course of dining room conversation. Everyone had seen us go into the woods. It seemed wise to make light of the venture.

Someone said that therapist was going to give up her job.

POOL balls.

Piano playing.

Bridge game.

A bridge game: "I sometimes think that guessing is tantamount to actually knowing what is in the partner's hand."

Bridge game: "Let's come out of this trance." A grand slam in no trumps, we could have bid.

An epileptic fit, Jackson man, clonic. Patients herded outside together. Led back to the pool and ping-pong room.

Trip to beach. A flirtation. French girl lies on beach and image is carved. Too much sunshine. I am deeply burned. Landing barges float around. I think about the invasion and talk it over with another patient.

Golden safety pin.

The Russians.

Back home.

Baldpate.

A morning of occupational therapy, peaceful, a swim.

An afternoon nap, the usual.

The movies. *Lady in the Dark.* Tears.

A dog at the corner (Maya's memory).

Lady in the Dark: so many parallels, the song she whis-
     tled, the childhood memory, courtroom, caged black
     beauty, the Christian girl, small and childish, gilded
     horse, so many parallels.

Dog at the corner.

The men weigh, standing with their backs to the scales,
     odor of paraldehyde.

We talk til late.

How to treat a depression.

"Kick in tail."

"Sexual stimulation."

"Dr. Schlomer would agree." How to instruct youngsters
     about sex til 3 a.m.

"Don't talk about your symptoms."

I leave the tennis game without comment, go and take
     my bath.

(The drip, drip, drip and drop, drop, drop, all night, Sat-
     urday).

(Homophiliac complex!)

Harry excited, why?

Dinnertime I am quiet.

After dinner.

Bridge.

Early a.m. After breakfast, walk to edge of estate and back.

Betty: "I'm only to trying to save your life." Night before. Mrs. Houston.

ON my second Sunday at Baldpate, nine days after my arrival, I was sitting on the lawn with several patients. It was late in the morning. A patient walked up and said something to me. This remark led me to get up and go to my room on some errand. As I walked along the driveway, I saw Vivian Tillotson and her little daughter, getting out of their car. Vivian was the wife of my friend, the psychiatrist Dr. Kenneth Tillotson, who had presided over my care at McLean hospital. I walked up to her.

"Hello, Vivian," I said.

"Hello, Perry," she replied as she came forward. "Kenneth came out here on consultation and we drove out with him. We thought that we would just wander around the place."

"I have to go inside for a few minutes but I'll join you later if I may."

I went inside and attended to some minor matter in my room. I must have been standing at the wall mirror combing my hair when Dr. Kenneth Tillotson came down the corridor following one of the Baldpate doctors. The door was opened and I could see him clearly as he walked along. He looked serious, nervous and tense, perhaps because of the consultation he had ahead of him. When he looked at me, he did not smile.

"Hello, Kenneth," I said.

"Oh hello, Perry," came Kenneth's reply. He walked on hurriedly, not stopping to shake hands.

"I hope I'll have a chance to see you later before you go."

He disappeared out the back door.

Outside, I found Vivian and her little daughter and we sat in some chairs beneath a tall tree looking toward the lake. We talked about minor subjects as they rippled into our rather light conversation. After a while we went out back and sat in the swing. The Tillotson child sang some new songs that had become popular, such as "Don't Sweetheart Me."

Kenneth came up and greeted me in a friendly way.

"May I talk with you for just a minute or two?" I asked.

"Surely, Perry," he replied. "Take more time than that."

We moved away from his wife and daughter and sat on the grass beneath a tree. I told him about some of the experiences that led up to my attack. I expressed appreciation for some of the features of his previous care of my case, complimented him upon his advice about getting an adequate sexual outlet, a subject neglected by other psychiatrists.

"If I have ever said anything about you that may have been a source of misunderstanding between us," I said, "please give me a chance to explain before you bear judgment against me."

Kenneth rose suddenly. After a friendly farewell between us all, he departed with his family.

"Don't be in any hurry to leave here," Vivian said.

"Come along Vivian," Kenneth interjected. He spoke a little sharply, as if to imply, "Perry needs to get back to a normal life." If Kenneth meant this, he was quite correct, because a return to the normal walks of life would have saved me calamities and many months of suffering.

As they drove away, I went in to dinner. There was only one seat left and this was next to Emma. An especially good steak meal was being served.

"We are very glad to have you here," said an elderly woman on my right.

ONE morning, I was sitting in front of the cottage with four or five women patients; included were Emma, the Houston woman, the French woman, and Betty Winn. It was a beautiful spring day with the sun shining down with a beautiful flood of sunbeams.

"Dr. Baird, we are sun worshippers too," the Houston woman said to me.

Dr. Cohen came along and went inside with one of the women patients. He came out after about twenty minutes.

"It's warm in there," he said to us.

It was a warm day inside and out. What did he mean? The statement didn't really make much sense.

As we all sat there talking, all the women were acting a little strangely. Each of them was playing with her jewelry as she talked and there seemed to be some definite association between the type of comment and some gesture such as rotating a ring or adjusting a bracelet. Here they may have been trying to teach me a sign language, or it may have just meant nothing.

———

ONE night dancing, I was with the hostess. The pool table was empty of balls. Harry and the young Texas girl were dancing on one side of the table. Three balls appeared: red, green and blue. The pool balls had been laid out and were in some special order. I forget the details. Mr. Denis sat on the pool table, swinging one leg. The man with the hearing aid was sitting facing the corner of table next to Mr. Denis. He had some old magazines, including an ancient copy of *The New Yorker.* There was an illustration: a vast estate; a marble staircase; a wealthy man, fat and sad, sitting at the bottom; a vast green lawn; a lawn mower. Mr. Denis began shifting the blue, green and red balls around, in a peculiar suggestive manner. I tried very hard to figure out the meaning of this peculiar puzzle. Could the green pool ball mean the wealthy class, the blue ball the aristocrats and the red ball, communistic? I didn't know. My imagination ran wild.

While conversing with these two, I used the term "Cue-tips" without any special meaning. In my office I use pre-pared applicators—wooden sticks with cotton tips—called "Q Tips." Near the pool table were some steel braces to be used in gluing on those velvet pads called "cue tips" which the hostess had pointed out to me and referred to by this term.

The next day, as I sat at the piano, Mr. Denis came along.

"What did you mean when you said 'Q Tips' last night?" he asked.

"Oh," I said. "Do you mean in reference to that 'crap' about the pool balls?"

He looked surprised, turned and left the room. It was

after this that some of the patients began to get rough in their remarks to me.

A state trooper came in and mingled with nurses and patients for a while. I found that he was a very pleasant kind of officer and fun to talk with. I asked to see his handcuffs and put them on. They happened to be exactly like the ones used to take me to Westborough. It was interesting to study the automatic tightening mechanism. As one struggles in them, they are apt to close more tightly on the wrist.

"How are you taught to shoot nowadays?" I asked the officer. "Do you use the technique of Wyatt Earp?"

The officer and the nurse were standing there. Both looked surprised and uneasy. The term "Wyatt Earp" must have sounded a little crazy to them. I went on to explain.

"Wyatt Earp was a frontier marshal. He carried two guns given to him by the Wells Fargo express. He shot from the hip and aimed just below the middle of the abdominal region, a large target and a very effective target."

The officer and nurse looked a little relieved when I was able to translate my original statement into language easily understandable to them.

I wandered out through the back door and found the police cruising car still there.

"This reminds me of the time the bear came in to the bathroom," I heard the French woman say.

I went into the kitchen and found the nurse making coffee for the policeman. I talked with the officer about hours and wages. I found that he had many interesting things to say. I expressed my views regarding hours and wages for local and state police and how their services might be improved by more favorable working hours and high wages, enabling the public to employ a better type of man.

The French woman came wandering through the kitchen.

"This reminds me of the time the bear came in to the bathroom," she said again as she left the kitchen.

I went to bed but lay awake thinking and wondering about so many things. The police cruising car stood outside, its radio picking up many messages from headquarters. The car must have stayed outside the window of our room until 3 a.m.

Monday morning was uneventful. After lunch, Emma, the French woman, Betty and I were sitting back of the little cottage, talking. Betty laughed. Somehow this made me mad. A tennis game was suggested. Emma and I played Betty and the French woman. My game rose to top form. My smashing serves fell into corners of the serving courts and were seldom returned. My aggressive game, especially my tornado serve, had evidently awakened the attention of several patients who usually watched us play. One by one they left. Did they sense my anger? Did they think I was unduly upset?

MARY Lou Lee—checker game
Two red chickens out in front. Danger, danger, danger.
Nurse, I and Mary Lou walk in the moat, walk and run.
10 p.m. to bed. I sleep until about midnight, ask for amytal, take one or two doses, awake at 4:30 or 5 a.m.,
  get up and talk with nurse and attendant.
Toward breakfast time, I am showing the attendant
  wrestling and jiu-jitsu, many holds not in the books.

Mary Lou comes out.

Breakfast.

Morning, outside, Jewish attendant, and several Jewish patients around. Someone hands me a newspaper clipping with headline: "Jewish women seek U.S.
port."

I sit with them on grass and say, "The trouble with this
world is that there's not enough of the spirit of tolerance and forgiveness," and I talk on in this vein.

A Jewish seamstress comments: "I never believed in four
leafed clovers before. I found one yesterday."

Lunch.

Afternoon nap.

Afternoon on lawn.

Dinner.

Early evening on lawn.

Radio, much talk about invasion of the Continent by al-
lies.

TUESDAY morning, eleven days after my arrival at Baldpate, I was up early as usual, sitting in the swing, rocking
back and forth. Betty Winn came out of the rear entrance
of the main building and walked toward me. I got up and
went over to her and walked at her side as she went over to
the hospital where she took her insulin treatments.

"This is serious," she said as we walked along.

"What do you mean, Betty?"

"I can read minds too," said Betty. "It's easy."

We walked on in this view for four or five minutes. Betty,

a perfectly sensible girl usually, seemed to be trying to say something to me, but seemed obliged to clothe her language in such a way as to conceal her purposes from the others, in case I should quote her statements. Or perhaps she was just trying to reach me by suggestion or reference. I could not understand her. At the hospital, she gave me a cigarette. We both smoked a few minutes and then she went in the hospital and I walked back to my swing.

After breakfast, I wandered around and at about 9 a.m. the Houston woman came out of the old inn building. I joined her and walked to the occupational therapy unit. As we entered, the therapist turned to me.

"Don't come in here!" she said to me abruptly and in a loud, high-pitched voice. "You're dressed up to go swimming." I was merely dressed in an ordinary sort of clothes. What could she have meant? I turned and walked away. The idea of going down to the lake appealed to me. I wanted to be alone. I went down the driveway to the road and walked along toward the lake. An attendant came alongside of me in his car and stopped. We talked.

"Do you suppose it is all right for me to go down to the lake?" I asked.

"Better get permission," he said.

I turned around, went back to the main building, climbed the stairs to the second floor and found the nurse in charge at the nurse's office.

"May I go down to the lake?" I asked.

"Do you feel well?" she asked. "You've been looking flushed and upset."

"I feel just fine. I just thought I'd like to go down to the lake."

"It's alright to go to the lake, but don't go in swimming."

"Thank you very much," I said and went back to the road. The attendant was still waiting in his car.

"I obtained permission to go to the lake," I remarked as I passed his car. I followed the road down to the lake, got on the path on the far side of the lake and walked deep into the woods. I wanted to be alone, away from the constant riddle and annoyance of things other patients were saying to me.

I crossed a road and went on and on, staying in the woods. I came to a little house by the highway and found that I could not go on except by following the main highway or by going on in a wooded section heavily overgrown with thickets. I knocked on the door of the house, a new one just built, and asked to use the telephone. I wanted to get a taxi to go back to the hospital, thinking that I may have been gone a little too long and that I should hasten back. It's true also that I would have loved to climb in a taxi and leave the state.

Baldpate Hospital, 1944

The patient got on fairly well at the "Inn" until June 6, 1944, when he left the premises without authorization, visited a farm and waded in a lake nearby. He was apprehended and returned to Baldpate where he seemed confused in supplying details of his expedition. A few days later he

began to be irritable, demanding, surly and restless. With a menacing grimace he stated, "What
were the bitter pills they have been giving me?
If you are giving me the wrong medicine somebody
is going to get into trouble."

CHAPTER ELEVEN

I n his records, it is noted that while at Baldpate hospital my
father "destroyed two iron hospital beds, broke the panels of
his room, and threatened to strike the nurses." Only two weeks
after his admittance to Baldpate, his behavior was deemed too
unruly for the hospital's standards, and he was transferred without delay back to Westborough.

Westborough State Hospital, 1944

June 10

The patient cooperated well on being returned
to our hospital. He came back dressed in a Palm
Beach suit, brown shoes, made a very excellent
appearance and came back to the hospital accom-
panied by two State Troopers, one on either side,
carrying his large brown suitcases. He readily greeted the writer and was friendly. He was
slightly over-talkative, but not too much so.
When he was asked what happened, he stated it
was all a misunderstanding, tried to maintain he
had not attempted to escape from Baldpate, that
one of the Doctors had given him permission to
go down by the lake, that this Doctor had gone
on vacation and those left in charge thought
he overstepped his privileges. It happened on
two occasions. He stated that each time the
car picked him up he was on his way back to the

hospital. "I would not be going in that direction if I was trying to escape," he stated.

June 13

This patient is quiet, cooperative and adjusting well. He spends considerable time writing and does some reading. He readily indulges in conversation. He does seem slightly tense. At times he tries to be very jovial. One of the jokes he tried to make was really rather sensuous and he made this even though a female nurse was standing in the group. He himself laughed more at it than the others. He still tends to show euphoria and shows no depression. There really have been no gross changes in this patient's condition since his return to the hospital. In fact, the writer feels that his condition is the same as it was for a few weeks before he left our hospital to go to Baldpate.

June 30

The writer today served the notification to the patient that his "license was revoked" by the Board of Registration in Medicine as of June 21st, 1944, at least it was voted such at a meeting on that date. The patient was ordered to remove all of his signs, public displays etc. and to no longer receive money for the practice of medicine. The original was given to the patient and the writer signed a copy that he had been served the original. This was notarized and returned to the Board of Registration in Medicine. Patient had little to say. He did, after

reading the notice, want to know if it was tem-
porary or permanent and he immediately wrote a
letter to his lawyer.

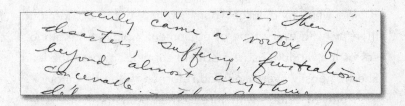

THREE weeks after my readmission to Westborough, I was
sitting on the grass next to the Proctor building when Dr.
Boyd walked toward me.

"I have very bad news for you," he said. He handed me
a letter.

In technical language the letter directed me to appear
before the Board of Registration and to provide reasons why
my medical license should not be suspended, cancelled or
revoked on grounds of insanity, according to section, etc. etc.

Immediately I wrote a letter to my lawyer, Mr. Dodge,
asking him to arrange for me to be at the hearing. As I
wrote, I stated two strong intuitions:

1. Dr. Lang will not let me go to the hearing.
2. My license will be revoked, no matter what happens.

Three or four days later, my lawyer wrote: "Impossible
to arrange for you to be at hearing."

———

ONE morning, two and a half weeks after readmission, I
went with the occupational therapist nurse to the library. A
patient came in holding a little robin that had just hatched
out. She found it on the grass. It could not find its nest.

We went to a large room, equipped for occupational
therapy, with every type of equipment. I played the piano. I
sat at the window. I saw a patient running towards the lake.
She was easily overtaken and returned to the dormitory.

I played bridge with three other patients in the afternoon. We ate candy and drank cold drinks. I overheard the
girl say that she put the little robin back on the grass. She
came along later and found it half-eaten by a cat.

Bridge was over. We returned the tables and chairs to
the nurses' house from which we had brought them.

Dr. Boyd arrived.

"You have been transferred to another ward," he said.
"Your things have already been sent over."

I felt a little happy.

MY lawyer wrote that he appeared before the Board of
Registration and they made it clear that revocation of my
license was the most we could expect. My lawyer went on
to say the license had been revoked. The news did not surprise me and I did not feel deeply shocked.

Routine notices began to appear. There were instruc-
tions to notify medical societies and hospitals that my license had been revoked; to withdraw my name from the
telephone book, the directory listing in my building, and
from the door of my office.

My secretary wrote that patients could no longer be accepted in my name. When answering the telephone the girls say, "Hello" instead of, "This is Dr. Baird's office."

Gretta wrote that she couldn't see me for six months on account of Massachusetts divorce laws.

The agony of these activities did not upset me in any outward sense, but my heart was slowing breaking.

ON Sunday, Dr. Boyd came to make a visit, one week or so after my transfer. He seemed surprised and inquisitive that I was not visibly upset over the revocation of my license.

"The proper viewpoint is to make up your mind to get your license back again," he advised.

I hadn't asked for his advice. I could see no other possible viewpoint to take, except to give up all hope, to surrender to defeat and mediocrity.

Dr. Boyd couldn't seem to comprehend why I didn't get manic or deeply depressed over the question of my license. I bore up well. I did so on purpose, perhaps through pride, perhaps because I had expected it, perhaps because I had been through so much that I expected nothing but hard luck and continued reversals. I had all the courage, fight and stamina necessary to face my problem. I didn't need for Dr. Boyd to advise me, to take a viewpoint that has long been natural for me: to struggle and fight.

Boyd did most of the talking. He proceeded to give me a vast amount of unsolicited advice, dishing it out as if it were something that would straighten out my affairs very nicely. He spoke in a confident manner, as if he thought I'd been yearning for his help, as if I were greatly complimented to have him take the time to talk with me. I had not sought his advice; I did not want it. His advice was based upon little thought about my problem and very little knowledge of my case. He sat there confident, overbearing, fat, stupid, his mustache wriggling up and down. On and on he talked. He spoke with pride about the Westborough State Hospital.

"About all we have to offer here is a regular life for our patients," he said, as if Westborough had some magic to offer.

Oh, dear God, I say to anyone who cares to listen: Westborough State Hospital and other places like it have nothing to offer; nothing but a jail-like incarceration, brutality and ugliness. The patients who come here recover not because of the treatment they receive, but in spite of it. Some are submerged by it, die of it.

Boyd continued. He referred to the acute stage of my recent illness. He commented with sarcasm upon some of the things I'd said, my references to cosmic rays, my illusion concerning the yellow wall paint that I referred to as "riboflavin." He gave his interpretation of the manic psychosis and emphasized speed of thought and action as factors to reckon with. I complimented him on this and said I preferred his interpretation to the usual one.

"What is the usual one?" he asked.

"Oh, most authorities just think of the manic psychosis as a state characterized by loss of inhibition," I explained.

"But that's just a description of what happens, not interpretation," he commented.

I had flattered him. He puffed up a little. I'd wanted to

keep peace with him. I disliked him heartily. Oh to get rid of him! But no, he was having a fine time. He dictated on how I was to manage my life in order to remain free of trouble. He proposed to solve this problem that no one has ever solved before:

"Lead a regular life, eat and sleep regularly," Boyd said. "Have sexual intercourse about three times per week. Reduce your income to $15,000 per year. Don't overwork. When you feel yourself getting manic, just don't talk so much . . ."

In general, he proposed that I just remember the symptoms and overcome them.

This interview with Boyd was an endless affair.

"You have a better brain than mine," he went on.

"I'm not so sure," I replied, shuddering to think that my brain could deteriorate to a level with his.

"Oh yes," said he. "You have a better command of the general field of medicine."

He knew nothing of my talents and my shortcomings. He was not qualified to compare.

Boyd also seemed to think I was happy about my divorce.

"I'm not so sure that I *am* happy about it," I said.

"Aren't you relieved to have your freedom, to be able to live as you choose?"

"I'm not entirely sure!"

"Of course, you know, the manics run the world," Boyd continued. He developed this thesis along the usual lines.

If he really thinks that manics are useful enough to run the world, I wondered to myself, then why do they keep me here at Westborough, on and on, when I am normal?

"Well, I might have done this sooner for you," Boyd concluded, condescendingly. "I thought it would be better to wait until now, when you'd benefit more."

Somehow the interview ended.

He spoke one last time about my revoked license.

"Of course, you know, it will take months to get it back."

I had never listened to advice less welcome.

CHAPTER TWELVE

Westborough State Hospital, 1944

July 3

The patient carries on a good conversation that is relevant and coherent. He did show a little grandiose trend in his flow of thoughts, namely about his practice being $50,000 or $60,000 gross and carrying approximately that amount of life insurance, talked of his debts of $18,000, all of which figures he spoke of, not fully realizing their true value. However, at the present time, he has a much better sense of values in general, talking more of supporting his children, and paying his alimony. Also he listened when being spoken to, he is not as talkative as he was preceding going to Baldpate and for a short time after his return to Westborough. His conversation is good. He shows no gross abnormalities of mood. He does tend to joke a little more than he did. He seems to see things in a more humorous sense but he is not euphoric. He did show a little tenseness for the week or two after returning from Baldpate, but this too has subsided. He is showing no depression.

In a moment of intense concentration upon phases of mental unhappiness past

THE days at Westborough State Hospital were now growing more and more oppressive. The food was becoming increasingly distasteful to me. The full reality of what it meant to have my license revoked began to gnaw away great raw holes in my soul. The usual seven and a half hours of sleep that we were permitted did not seem enough. It felt good to lie down for a little while after breakfast and again after lunch. The first day I did this, Miss Hayward, the nurse, was off-duty and no one seemed to object to my taking this extra rest. The next morning, I ate breakfast, swept the upper floor, collected the dirt in dustpans and disposed of it, then washed up and went to lie down. I had scarcely closed the door to my room when in came Miss Hayward's voice and footsteps.

"Where is Dr. Baird?" she asked. "I miss him!"

I went to the door and told her that I'd be out in just a moment.

During subsequent days, I tried to get a little extra rest. Every time I made the attempt, Miss Hayward came storming to my door (a three-bed room) and, without knocking, opened it loudly and commanded me to come downstairs. At every provocation she would behave as if I were some juvenile delinquent and she an officer empowered to treat me as roughly as possible. These experiences with Miss Hayward were very upsetting, although I admit I shouldn't have let her or anything she said bother me—no matter how she said it.

One hot day, I was lying there after lunch, trousers off.

"Get on your pants and come downstairs!" she barked at me.

This desire for extra sleep was probably based upon the severe strain I was under. The revocation of my license itself had not made me ill, but the actual procedure of notifying hospitals and medical societies—so that they could eliminate my name as a physician connected with them—and all the details of this humiliating procedure were an ordeal ranking as a horror with death itself.

It seemed so absurd to revoke my license. I was locked up securely at Westborough and couldn't get a release to return to my practice until every proof of my recovery was at hand. All they accomplished by revoking my license was to:

1. Make it difficult for my assistant to hold my practice together.
2. Create publicity unfavorable to the continuation of my practice.
3. Make it impossible for my assistant to carry on in my name.
4. Jeopardize the future of my practice by causing undesirable publicity regarding my illness.
5. Create difficulties carrying medical protection insurance and resuming it, after recovery.

6. Hardships and embarrassments, but not an iota accomplished in the direction of protecting the public from getting my services while sick.

What pain to have your name as a practicing physician removed from the roster of all Massachusetts hospitals, directories, medical societies and other institutions. To have your old reliable secretary who was holding things together discharged by another doctor. What pain to have your assistant discontinue using your prescription pads and stationery, and instead to use his own.

The days seemed long. I read my mail and kept up my correspondence, enjoying the daily newspapers and reading books. There were visitors only rarely and the few who came stayed only for short periods of time. There was no opportunity for any real exercise. During certain hours of the morning and afternoon, we were allowed to sit outside in front of the dormitory. There was a stone bench beneath a day shade tree and chairs were available. You were permitted to amuse yourself by putting rubber horseshoes (quoits), throwing a baseball or walking around a small plot of grass. The rules required that you confine your activities to very small space with clear vision of the nurse or attendant in charge. If you tried to walk enough to get any real exercise, you would appear to be over-active. Most patients just sat around or lay on the grass. There was no amusement of any regular sort. Once or twice a week, some of us were taken to the auditorium for music and dancing. These excursions were irregular and brief. There was no bowling.

In this atmosphere of boredom, loneliness, uselessness, my own little world had come to an end. I was divorced from my wife. I was coming to the realization of what it meant to have a family broken up. I hadn't seen my children even once since I came to Westborough. My own profession had been taken away from me. The clouds were black and I saw no silver lining.

In a moment of intense concentration upon phases of marital unhappiness past and present, I could look upon divorce as a logical solution. But as my mind took time to consider all details of the situation, I realized that divorce meant the loss of certain things mutually possible in marriage, not otherwise available to either marital partner. No longer a home with children, moments enjoyed with mutual friends now to be discarded; the meaning of Christmas, birthdays, just a warm and welcome place to return at the end of the day; a wife to plan parties at home and to accept invitations elsewhere, talks with my wife at the end of the day, local gossip, kissing the children goodnight and tickling them to make them laugh, bedtime stories; the question of little comforts, laundry, dry cleaning, all the little things which make up a home, the club we enjoyed together.

Divorce is a horrible nightmare, but just a part of the great general nightmare of failure, frustration, loss of license to practice, a long and expensive illness, the torrent of disgrace and loss of prestige in the community, so many things that in retrospect now seem preventable, yet actually could they have been?

The longings of the human heart are changeable and elusive. The good fortune we enjoy today may not be appreciated until it has been taken away and we have to fight and try to get it back.

AFTER my return to Westborough from Baldpate, I stayed there quietly, peacefully in perfect cooperation and in quite normal health for a month. During these weeks, I experienced the torment and realization that I had been transferred to a decent private hospital, Baldpate, and had had a chance to finish my sentence under comfortable circumstances. As I look back on that experience I can find no meaning in what happened. It was at Baldpate that I had been subjected to strange treatment by the other patients. There must have been some purpose in the upsetting situation to which I was subjected in inconsiderate fashion, but I cannot fathom it. I had foreseen that upsetting experiences would arise at Baldpate. I intended to ignore them, to be calm, courteous and cooperative. It was depressing to realize that my foresight and my conscious effort had come to nothing. I should not have permitted anything that happened to interfere with my peace of mind and I really don't know why I did not maintain spiritual equanimity.

For a while I helped dry the dishes. I was at first glad to have something to do. Gradually it became a disgusting experience. Many of the dishes came through with large amounts of food adhering to them. The usual procedure was just to wipe off the food with the towel. Knives, forks,

HE WANTED THE MOON   133

and spoons came through in a similar condition and were treated in the same way. The food itself was sickening and my ability to eat it grew less each day. After wiping dishes for a while and finding how filthy they really were, it became increasingly difficult to face a meal.

My hands began to develop dryness and a beginning rash from the soap left on the dishes. I asked permission to stop helping with dishes.

"No one is compelled to do any work at all around here," the attendant replied.

And yet it was obviously true that it is the patients mostly that run the hospital.

The whole chain of events from February 20 to early July, almost five months of unending disasters, was a little more than I could view without feeling appalled. On days when I smoked too much, I became deeply depressed. During these weeks at Westborough, remorse and discontent ran deeply. There were few visitors. Letters continued to arrive, though in much less volume than before. They brought scant comfort and my few brief visitors did not relieve my loneliness and sense of failure.

I CONTINUED my duties: sweeping the upstairs floor, drying the dishes during the men's week for this, sitting around, minding my own business.

The desire to escape became strong, but I did not give into it without weighing all the considerations and precautions. I gathered as much information as I could get. I was quiet, said very little except what was expected of me from a viewpoint of common courtesy. My activities were restricted to a peaceful and unobtrusive walking about. I read a great deal and slept as much as the hospital would allow. Without complaint I had swept the floors and dried the dishes. I had showed no upsets such as anger and was at peace with everyone. I was in perfectly normal shape, maintaining absolutely normal activities in all respects. Yet I knew that they had strange ways of judging your condition.

One day, Dr. Boyd stopped to talk with me.

"You are less active than you were," he commented.

He seemed to imply that I was still manic. Actually I was normal, but if anything else, slightly depressed. To find yourself so carelessly misjudged in matters so vital to your future welfare is a source of much misgiving. You are at the mercy of the most casual, ruthless doctors who have it within their power to destroy your entire career on the basis of judgments entirely whimsical in nature, opinions arrived at by the most casual and haphazard lines of observation and reasoning: an unhappy set-up for the poor defenseless patient.

I began to reason about the problem of escape:

1. It would be difficult to accomplish. Recapture was likely and incarceration would be greatly prolonged. While on the grounds it would be easy to start running, but with other patients, nurses, and attendants watching constantly, it would be rather easy for them to catch you before you left the grounds or got far beyond them.
2. Escape would complicate matters in many ways,

handicap my friends in their efforts to help me, create a problem of making peace with Westborough again, put off longer the day of returning to my practice.

3. Escape might turn friends, relatives and professional associates against me.

On the other side of the ledger I was able to marshal a formidable and convincing array of thoughts:

1. Dr. Lang—both stupid and conservative—seemed to be afraid to let me leave, unwilling to take the responsibility. If I departed, behaved normally, got checkups with other psychiatrists as well as friends and relatives, proved by my conduct outside that I was entirely normal, it would be easier for Lang. As long as I stayed at Westborough, it would remain impossible for him to predict what would happen to me after discharge. If I returned, supported by evidence of recovery, he would have no reasonable alternative but to release me. I could, in other words, get approbation and protection from agents and agencies outside of Westborough and then return in hope of getting things straightened out.

2. Dr. Boyd had implied that my further stay might be a matter of months in spite of my good recovery.

3. Miss Hayward had given me the hint that I might be kept there a long time, merely because I could pay the maximum of $10 weekly.

4. I knew that my psychiatrist friends, Drs. Fleming and MacPherson, might come to see me soon and would

try to get me out or get me transferred elsewhere. I felt that, despite their efforts, further delays would ensue.

5. I was influenced by a desire to get away from everything, to escape not only from Westborough but also from the whole world that I'd known, to start anew, anywhere, doing anything, vanish forever. I did not want to die. I was just tired of pain, force, jail, rough treatment. The story I've told so far contains an account of the usual modern care of my condition. I believe such measures are destructive. They contribute handicaps, they hurt, they insult, they injure, they shackle, they take away freedom, they impair recovery; they are barbaric products of pure force; they are uncivilized, they reek, they stink.

6. I was growing depressed, less and less able to endure the food, the boredom, the limitless accumulation of disasters. I feared a real depression might take hold of me; that my stay at Westborough would go on from one year to the next and that I would never get a chance to get back to normal life and make an adjustment to it. I was being harmed badly by two little men, Boyd and Lang. I felt that there was grave danger to my sanity if I stayed here. If I fled it would be in self-defense.

7. As I took account of my position, it was clear that everything had been taken away: my profession, my family, I'd lost many friends, my money was gone. It didn't seem that I could make matters much worse by leaving. There was a chance that I might make them

better. There was nothing very great to lose; everything to gain. The gods seemed to beckon to me. I could hear the answer in the wind that seemed to call me to take matters into my own hands.

8. Remarks by both patients and nurses suggested that some of them hoped I would run away. They knew so much that they'd never tell. It was sometimes impossible to abide by their hints and suggestions.

The instant planned for escape seemed to be at hand. It was after suppertime and everything was relatively quiescent. The doctors had gone home and the day shift of nurses and attendants had departed, to be replaced by the relatively smaller night shift. Clearly there was no automobile that could be used to pursue me and there were no state patrol cars in sight. The coast seemed clear and entirely favorable, but it might change at any minute.

The attendant in charge was sitting at the edge of the lawn with his back to me. He was completely diverted by his conversation with other patients and some hospital employees. An elderly patient on parole, one of those trusted with supervising groups of patients while they were on the lawn, was sitting quietly in his chair, his left side toward me. He was looking off in the distance. I was standing about twenty-five yards away, walking casually among a group of six or eight patients.

The weather was favorable. I had figured out a reasonable plan. For many days, I gauged distances and studied every detail of the hospital routine that might play a part. I had made a careful mental calculation and had charted a course to include running between two particular trees, crossing a road, then going to the right of a small brick building and then to the main highway by going along the rear of a row of houses located along the driveway leading to the hospital. I knew that immediately after I started running, my intentions would become evident to many others and the machinery for capturing me would be put into effect. This would include sending out a searching party of attendants and male nurses and would involve notification of the state police who would surround and search the section of woods into which I had disappeared. It seemed wise not to plan more than a few hours ahead. It would be necessary to feel my way along, step by step.

I had been walking in a circle for about ten minutes trying to formulate final plans and to observe every detail of the surrounding circumstances of the moment. I came to a stop at the top of the lawn, next to the driveway in front of the brick dormitory. I turned around to make one last careful inspection and then I moved slowly toward the two trees marking the line of travel that I had chosen. I stopped for a moment beneath a large tree. My heart was racing and pounding as I have seldom felt it do before. I wondered: am I afraid of some unseen development that my intuition knows about but my mind does not grasp? Does my heart tell me that I am about to do a foolish and risky thing? At this moment of indecision, I reacted emotionally against the sense of fear and a feeling of proud defiance rose in my breast.

A sudden gust of wind blew through the branches above

me and made two successive coughing sounds that seemed to say to me, "Go ahead!"

Instantly I broke into a run, as fast as I was capable of. I felt as if I were traveling on winged feet. The distance between the start and my destination in the woods seemed to fly by in an instant.

CHAPTER THIRTEEN

Westborough State Hospital, 1944

Escaped. It was reported to the writer today
that this patient left from the lawn in front of
Talbot West. He was not actually seen going but
was reported missing about an hour later. Search
of the grounds and highways was unsuccessful. A
telegram was later sent to his wife. The Superintendent was notified, he advised this. The police
were not notified at this time. A telegram was
also sent the following day notifying the father
of the escape. Dr. Lang in turn received a reply
from this. The writer received calls from the
patient's Secretary, who stated that the telegram had been sent to her, and she in turn would
contact the wife who was in Maine for the summer.

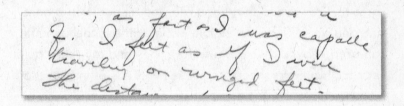

AFTER crossing the highway, I ran down an embankment
and into the wooded area. I was breathless, heart pounding wildly, weak from overexertion. My feet sank into the
soft earth beneath me and slowed my progress to a walk.
Ahead of me lay a mass of underbrush, fallen trees, pools

of mud and water, a hopeless tangle of vegetation so dense that travel through it was tedious, slow, painful and fatiguing. To save time I climbed upon fallen tree trunks and would run the length of them unless they gave way beneath my weight.

So fierce was my desire to avoid capture, so desperate was my fear of it, that I plunged headlong into dense bushes and crawled through them on hands and knees. There was no time for any thought except toward the goal of getting away from Westborough and into a normal environment. Quickly I became covered with scratches, bruises and insect bites and the palms of my hands carried deeply embedded splinters. None of these discomforts seemed to penetrate my consciousness. No amount of pain or discomfort seemed too great a price to pay.

After traveling a distance of two or three hundred yards from the road into this wooded quagmire—in what might have been only twenty-five or thirty minutes but what seemed like hours—I arrived at an area of dense undergrowth. I concluded that I had reached a spot even a hunting dog would find inaccessible. I dug a little tunnel beneath an area heavily overgrown with bushes and lay there quietly for two hours, heedless of the hundreds of insects that attacked face, neck, hands, wrists and ankles and even bit me through the thin coverings of trousers, shirts and socks.

After dark, the many birds stopped singing and all became very still. I had heard human voices from a distance but these had disappeared. All was quiet now, exceedingly quiet, and I felt safe in continuing my journey. Only the early shades of darkness had fallen and I could still see well enough to find my way along without making too much noise. After getting beyond the tangled mass of dead trees, bushes, and the soft mushy ground, I came upon a more normal section of forestland with less dead trees and branches and with much firmer ground.

Travel then became faster, but every time I had traveled a short distance, I stopped and listened to make sure that I could not detect other footsteps nearby. The many small dead branches beneath my feet made loud crackling sounds and shut out all sounds coming from greater distances. It was no longer necessary to run. I walked slowly and without undue fatigue. For several miles I continued to stop every few paces, looking around to detect any moving object and listening for footsteps. My ears were strained to catch and interpret every sound.

I passed through the woods and reached an irrigation ditch flanked on each side by a growth of very high and tough sort of grass. This clearing had been cut through the forest region and it could be followed to the hills beyond the woods and toward Boston. By following the ditch I made faster progress, but every time my route carried me toward a house or even in the vicinity of a barking dog, I would change my direction and go back into the woods, taking wide turns to avoid any inhabited area. Finally I reached the hilly region. Leaving the irregular ditch and its high grass behind, I climbed over a fence at the foot of the first hill and slowly walked to the top, pulling myself along by holding on to small tree trunks and to the shrubbery.

Upon reaching the top of the first hill I felt once again very tired and, just before emerging from the trees, I lay down to rest. It was quite dark now, but a full, bright moon was coming up and the sky was filled with stars. As I lay there with the cool breezes blowing across my face and my eyes fixed upon the stars, I felt free again and happy. The happiness was a simple, animal-like, physical sensation, but it was not devoid of the consciousness of the many difficulties and uncertainties that lay ahead. Nor could I forget the haunting memories of nearly five months of almost intolerable suffering, the revocation of my license to practice and other realities. Yet here on the hillside I was happy in that simple, animal way; strangely happy just to be resting, cool and free of hospital barriers.

After a while I rose again and moved on. Travel was over stony ground but with wide areas of soft turf between the stones. It was possible to walk for a great distance at a good steady pace, guided by moonlight. I came to a rather high hillside, heavily overgrown with evergreen trees. When I reached the top, I looked back toward Westborough and thought I saw some lights flashing in the region of the swampy woodland where I had been hiding. I traveled over the hill and down on the opposite side which was extremely stony. After seeing lights in the woods, I began nervously to travel a little faster, even though the lights had been quite far away. As I came down the hill, I stumbled and fell several times. Once I jumped off the edge of a large rock and fell a distance of six to eight feet among some smaller rocks where I twisted one ankle but did not sprain it.

In passing through this section—heavily covered with small evergreen trees and stones of many sizes—my trousers became even more torn than was already the case. I

began to experience extreme thirst and became more uncomfortable in my desire for water. At this point, I reached
the bottom of the hill and came upon a small river spar-
kling in the moonlight. Trees grew close to the bank of the
river but stopped for a path that followed the river. At the
edge of the river, I lay face down upon a large, flat stone
and drank from the cool, clear water using my folded hands
as a cup. I followed this river for a long distance, drinking
more water occasionally.

After this I followed the railroad track that left the
course of the river and passed through a countryside of
fields, woods, low hills, all illuminated by the bright moonlight and all very beautiful. I had had very little exercise for
four and a half months and had become soft and decidedly
out of condition. At this time it must have been 10 p.m. or
11 p.m. and I was beginning to feel thirst again and great
fatigue. The sounds of a train became audible ahead of me
and in a few minutes the strong headlight of the train en-
gine became visible. The railway track was built at the top
of a high embankment. As the train came nearer, I ran down
the embankment, climbed through a barbed-wire fence and
lay face down in some high grass until the train had passed
slowly by.

A few feet away, surrounded on one side by trees, there
was a shallow pond in which many frogs were croaking their
moonlight songs. I removed my coat and laid it to one side,
rolled up my sleeves and lay down by the edge of the pond.
In my pocket were several letters. The envelope from one
of these was easily converted into a paper cup and from
this I drank greedily. The frogs were very near now and

they croaked noisily, evidently not disturbed by my presence. After a while I felt cooler and my thirst was almost completely satisfied. I drew away from the edge of the pond and lay in the high grass with my head on my coat and my eyes finding comfort in the stars above. I might have slept but for the swarms of insects which gathered. I covered my face with a handkerchief and lay my coat across my chest with my hands and wrists beneath it, but it did not seem to make much difference. Droves of mosquitoes and other insects found their ways into my ears, neck and ankles, inflicting their painful effects.

After a few minutes I wandered on, crossing through fields until I came upon a lonely road. Consistently, I adhered to the roadside fence and got well away from the road itself. With each passing car I felt a recurrent spasm of fear. In these instances, I merely lay face down in the ditch at the side of the road. My brown suit probably blended well with the general plan of camouflage and wasn't very noticeable in the moonlight. Had I been noticed by a state trooper cruising around, the police would surely have questioned me. Already I had made up a story to cover my situation, including the absence of a draft card and other forms of identification. I had intended to say that I was visiting friends in Worcester, that we had been at a party, that I had left my wallet in Worcester, that my friends had driven away as a joke when I got out of the car to empty my bladder. It was a tall story but I couldn't think of any other to explain my peculiar situation. If the police had driven me to Worcester, I had planned to have them leave me at the home of my friend Benjamin Alton and bluff my way out as best I could in the presence of the police, later explaining everything to Ben.

By now it was around midnight. I carried on. I was not at all familiar with the country in which I was traveling and I judged the direction of travel purely by an instinctive feeling as to whether it carried me farther and farther away from Westborough. I didn't greatly care whether I traveled north, east, south or west, so long as I left Westborough as far behind as possible. I was going to walk all night long and would conceal myself if necessary during the day. I had two dollars for a little food and some phone calls.

For one or two hours I traveled chiefly along a highway. The number of the highway meant nothing to me but I felt sure it led away from Westborough, either north or west. When possible I stayed off the highway itself, traveling through fields and just within the margin of wooded sections. I wasted a great deal of time wandering off the road in this way, but the highway was fairly well-traveled in spite of the hour of the night and it was a relief to get off the road and not to be compelled to duck away and hide from every passing automobile. After about twenty minutes the highway became clear of automobiles again and I set out to pass through the next town as quickly as possible. It was getting gradually lighter but dawn had not yet come. I came to some crossroads and looking up at a signpost I read these words: two miles to Westborough. At first I felt discouraged and blamed myself for being so stupid as to travel all night in a circle and end up so near the starting point, but later I grew assured at the idea and laughed to myself as I thought, "Well, at least this is the last place they would ever think of finding me."

For a mile or so I followed the road to Westborough, thinking that it would lead to the turnpike and that there I could pick up a ride to Worcester, but I changed my mind and turned back again, traveling over rocky hills and pasture land in order to be away from the Westborough road. As dawn came on Sunday morning, I passed through some small towns and came upon the old Boston Post Road and followed this for some distance. I stopped at some lodging houses thinking I might rent a room, bathe and get some sleep, but it was still quite early and no one would answer the front door bell.

I wandered into a dairy and watched the early morning milking of the cows. Then I came to a farmhouse just off the right side of the road. Walking into the barn, I was first welcomed by a friendly dog chained to his kennel inside, and then by a fine looking, cheerful farmer who proved to be most friendly.

"May I use your telephone?" I inquired.

"I'd be glad to have you use the telephone," he replied. "Just go into the house and you'll find it in the dining room next to the kitchen."

I thanked the farmer and went into the house. His wife was evidently upstairs asleep or dressing.

As I passed a mirror in the hallway, I took a good look at myself and wondered why the farmer had been so friendly. My face was covered with dried mud and my white shirt was conspicuously filthy. My hair was tousled and tangled; my suit was dirty, torn in many places, and the trouser legs were baggy. My shoes were caked with dirt and filth of many types. Stopping at the kitchen sink, I washed my face and combed my hair and straightened myself up as best I could. Then I went into the dining room and sat down to telephone. I was able to reach Larry Barnett who had done some work for me in the past. Many times he had trucked my horses around to various hunt clubs and shows. I reasoned that he probably knew nothing of my illness and might be willing to help. Evidently Larry was asleep. The telephone rang for a long time before he answered.

"Hello," said Larry sleepily and in a tone of evident annoyance.

"Sorry to wake you up, Larry," I said. "This is Perry Baird."

"Oh, hello, Doc."

"Say Larry, can you do some driving for me today?"

All arrangements were then completed for Larry to drive me for eight to ten hours in his car. It was agreed that I would pay $30 for the day's work. I gave Larry careful directions in regard to how to reach me. For the next hour, the farmer's family gathered for breakfast and they made me join them. I then took a short nap, paid for the phone calls and was sitting on the grass when Larry drove up. By this time, I had decided that my next destination would be Springfield.

My purpose in going to Springfield was to see my old friend, Leonard "Andy" Anderson, to ask him to help me.

I knew that, if he were in town, Andy would do so without hesitation. We set out for Springfield without telephoning and without worrying. I reasoned that Springfield would be a good direction in which to travel and, even if Andy were on vacation, I would at least be far enough away from Boston to reduce greatly the possibility of arrest. We made good time, leaving the farmhouse at about 9 a.m. and arriving in Springfield in about two and a half hours.

We stopped in front of Andy's house and Larry went to the door and rang the bell. Mrs. Anderson appeared at the door.

"Hello, Perry, come on in," she called out.

"I'd love to but my appearance is terrible," I replied. "Are you sure you won't mind?"

"I've been working in the yard and I'm in old clothes," she said. "Come on in. Andy has gone swimming with the children but he'll be back in a few minutes."

Larry was like an angel from heaven. He came back to the car and we made final business arrangements. We were good friends and he was willing to let me send him a check after reaching Dallas. He loaned me five dollars and let me borrow a pair of dark glasses. Just before driving away, Larry extended his hand and closed it upon mine in a warm, firm clasp of friendship. He looked straight at me and, from his facial expression, I could tell that he had some general idea of the problems that I'd had to face.

"Take good care of yourself, Doc," were his parting words.

Andy and his wife were the next angels to come along.

As I walked in the front door, Mrs. Anderson greeted me most warmly. We talked for a few minutes and she then suggested that I might like to take a bath while waiting for Andy to return. She took me to the guest room and showed me how to find the bathroom. She departed for a few minutes and then presently reappeared with a fresh suit of clothes, a clean shirt and some socks. It took quite a long time to take a thorough shower and to cleanse the tub afterwards. I cannot remember ever having been so dirty in my life. It felt good to get into clean clothes and once again to make a decent appearance. A tie that I had folded up and placed in my coat pocket had remained in good condition. My attire was quite satisfactory except for the absence of underwear. Nevertheless, I felt quite comfortable.

Mrs. Anderson and I sat and talked for a little while and soon thereafter Andy returned with the children. He was equally as cordial as his wife. I gave him a rather vague explanation about my clothes and so on, but he made things very easy by not asking any questions whatsoever. He brought out some very good Bourbon whiskey and mixed one good strong drink for each of us. We conversed amiably about his practice in Springfield, various aspects of dermatology and many other subjects of mutual interest. I told him of my ambition to become a writer and of the book I was engaged in writing. He offered considerable encouragement regarding the book and urged me to go ahead and submit the manuscript for publication without waiting too long to bring it to completion. He felt that I should not expect my first book to measure up to my own best ideals.

———

AFTER a delicious Sunday dinner, Andy and I drove to a nearby drugstore to buy some ice cream for dessert. On the way back, Andy turned to me.

"May I loan you some money?" he asked.

"That was most thoughtful of you, Andy," I replied. "I would appreciate it if you would either loan me some money or else cash a check for me."

I was indeed grateful to Andy for volunteering to loan me money. It was absolutely necessary for me to borrow some money from him and I hated to approach the subject. By opening the subject as he did, he saved me extreme embarrassment.

Andy's household was a happy, wholesome affair. The children frolicked around and one of them showed off some of her little tricks and did very well. I played a few simple tunes on the piano for them. They made me play one of them several times. Andy and I sat down in his study and talked about trains going west. He succeeded in getting me a Pullman reservation on a train leaving for Chicago at 4 p.m. I had arrived in Springfield toward the end of the morning, a veritable tramp, flat broke and covered with dirt. A few short hours later, I was immaculately dressed; I had ample cash in my pockets and a ticket to Chicago. Things were happening so fast, going so smoothly, that the whole experience seemed more like a dream than reality.

The train for Chicago was made up in Boston and I rather expected to encounter someone I recognized. There were a few familiar faces, but no one I felt sure that I knew.

At about 7 p.m. I went into the dining car and was seated at a table across from the first pretty girl I had seen since leaving Baldpate, and I ordered the second good meal I'd tasted since leaving Baldpate. I sat and ate slowly, letting my thoughts wander, not dwelling upon the many problems I knew lay ahead, thinking mostly of the pleasant sides of life. As I sat at the window watching the trees, hills and houses run by, I felt wave after wave of happiness, based upon a sense of freedom, a sense of escape, the knowledge that Westborough was left far behind and that the danger of being captured would be largely gone by the time I left New York State, in fact by the time of awakening on the following morning.

moves along strange paths.
we are only to such a
limited degree the pilots of
our souls it so

UPON arriving in Chicago I realized that I had the problem of finding a hotel room and of being able to get accommodations without a draft card or other forms of identification. The best plan seemed to involve calling a personal friend and asking him to put me up in some clubhouse or else give me an introduction to a hotel. By chance I had a good friend practicing psychiatry in Chicago. About ten o'clock on Monday morning, July 10, I stepped into a telephone booth and called Dr. Tom Fentress. He was most cordial and offered to see me immediately. I launched directly into an explanation of my problems. I left out the whole story of my stay in Westborough, my escape and my general predicament in Boston. I merely explained to him in general terms that I need his help in obtaining hotel accommodations in Chicago because I had no draft card. I explained that I had had episodes of manic-depressive insanity and that I was involved in litigation connected with my divorce, that I needed a letter testifying that my health was normal and that I hoped he felt my health was normal and that he could give me such a letter.

"What kind of a letter do you want and how would you like to have it worded?" Tom inquired. Whereupon I recited for him the kind of a letter I needed. He called his secretary and dictated to her a letter exactly corresponding to the one that I had detailed to him.

Tom was most hospitable in every respect. He arranged for me to stay at the University Club and he gave me a personal introduction so that use of a draft card would not be necessary. He requested that I be extended the usual check-cashing service of the University Club but finding that this had been discontinued he was very gracious in cashing me a check for fifty dollars. We had a most pleasant luncheon together at the University Club and we sat talking until the middle of the afternoon about many subjects of mutual interest. We discussed certain problems in neuropsychiatry. We discussed several phases of the treatment of the manic psychosis and the depressive psychosis. I was deeply interested to hear his views and he seemed very attentive to mine. We talked about schizophrenia in special reference to a classmate who has suffered from this disease.

By good fortune I succeeded in getting a reservation on one of the evening planes to St. Louis and I arrived there about 4 a.m. I was beginning to suffer intensely from one of the worst attacks of poison ivy I have ever seen. The weather was hot and I felt sticky and grimy from head to foot. The airport limousine took me to The Coronado Hotel and I was most pleased to be able to obtain a very comfortable room. I took a bath, using much soap and water on all areas of poison ivy and feeling much refreshed, I went to bed, sleeping soundly until about 10 a.m.

From my room at The Coronado Hotel in St. Louis I called my old friend Betty Bruce by telephone. She has known of my illnesses and she has seemed to understand them and forgive them more fully than anyone I know. It was good to hear Betty Bruce's voice and to have a personal conversation. I had written her from Westborough a long letter portraying the picture of my recent illness, relating the events leading up to the illness and depicting the sordid details of hospital conditions. She had not answered this letter and it had been some three months since I wrote to her. It was the kind of letter that a layman might not be able to digest and I feared that Betty must have been shocked, disillusioned or merely confused by the picture I painted.

"I didn't answer your letter because I didn't know whether I was supposed to write you or not," she explained. "Had I written I wouldn't have known what to say."

"The best way would have been just to write in a perfectly natural way, saying whatever you wanted to say," I replied. But I did not go on to make a long speech about letters to mentally ill people.

It was easy to discover that Betty Bruce had been deeply affected by my illness and our relations had been changed, perhaps passingly, perhaps forever. She did not invite me to Kansas City as she had done under similar conditions the year before.

After talking with Betty Bruce, a deep feeling of melancholia swept over me. I knew that something very dear to me had changed. The accumulated superstitions of our civilization in regard to insanity are very much still with us all and they can breed a devastating effect upon friendships, love and all relationships influenced by mental illness. I have been lucky in having suffered less than many from these superstitions. My attacks have usually been short and I have returned normal, healthy and able to make a living. By returning quickly to the normal associations with my friends, I have usually regained their confidence and respect before deep and lasting changes could take place. With Betty Bruce opportunities to see her are so few, that I can never hope to have a chance to rebuild our friendship upon the stable formation it has previously enjoyed.

And so I put down the telephone receiver with a heavy feeling in regard to the consciousness of a great loss, just part of the price to pay for this type of illness. The mentally ill patient is often treated like a criminal. His imprisonment and his case have many parallels to the situation of a criminal. Also he pays a similar price when he returns to society. He finds many things changed. With patience and courage he can earn back what he has lost, if time and circumstance do not operate too forcefully against him.

Most of my skin was a sorry mixture of a hideous, oozing poison ivy, cuts, splinters, bruises and deep excoriations, a reflection of the violence of my flight and the intrepid manner in which a soul desperate for freedom had dragged a body over miles of rough country. Yet I had obtained not the freedom I wanted but a sort of exile from the country I'd chosen to live in, woven with a new kind of loneliness, a longing for my family, my children, my home in Chestnut Hill, my practice, and all the things which I had to leave behind me in order to gain freedom from Westborough State Hospital.

The road ahead for me was going to be steeper than ever. I prayed for strength and courage to face the return trip, to face Lang and the Department of Mental Health, my friends, the Board of Registration, my practice, the people who saw me going into my last attack, the people who merely heard about the attack.

Later in the day, I was able to get comfortable Pullman accommodations on a train to Dallas. I was at this stage greatly fatigued, as a consequence of the accumulated experience of the journey, the inflammation of my skin, the constant burning and itching from my poison ivy. I boarded the train just after luncheon and arrived in Dallas on the following morning.

I telephoned my father. He had been notified of my escape and seemed relieved to hear my voice. He seemed glad to see me when I appeared at his office and he spoke in understanding terms of my escape. He had a certain comprehension of the difficulties that I had been through and he even seemed to admire my spirit in doing what I had done. He called Mother and told her happily of my arrival. I talked with Mother and arrangements were made for me to stay at home. Father commented upon how well I looked and how calm and stable I seemed. He seemed to think that I was more calm and stable than he had seen me in years.

I HAVE now been home in Dallas for over two months. During this time I have allowed myself to become rather lazy. I have developed the habit of sleeping from midnight to ten or eleven in the morning, even as late as two in the

afternoon. Once or twice I have slept all night and all the
following day. Last night I worked until ten thirty, writing the
account of my experiences—February 20 to July 8.

Here in Dallas, my thoughts grow reflective. They toil
with past events that cannot be changed. I eat, but I remain
both hungry and thirsty. So many errors in judgment and
behavior collect together to form a formable array of enemies striving to destroy the whole self, including that which
is good, useful, honorable and loyal. How can we separate
the bad self from the good without destroying both?

A phase of great strength, an ability to see things in light
of their happier aspects, the ability to rise above disgrace,
hardships, every type of defeat, to carry on with true courage, stamina, and fortitude, for months. And then again a
sort of lagging, warning a newer insight into events and people, an increased ability to see the distasteful side of certain
past events, and a compulsion to dwell upon them.

Despair—that mood which paralyzes thought and action and makes eternal sleep a goal and a prayer. I long
for the things I cannot have and for things that once were
mine and that have been taken away. I am a stranger in
a foreign land and I long to return to my home, my work,
my friends. What plan will fate unfold? To stay here idle,
to waste valuable time, to be caught in the locks of a trap
whose fabrication I took part in? Oh save me, God, from despair and hopelessness, save me for a happy and useful
life, spare me from uselessness and boredom, give me a
job, a home, my children.

Oh God, what new destinies lie ahead, what new hard-
ship, disappointments, tragedies, success are in store? Surely

happiness will come again and depart again. Oh God, I need your help. I do not want to die. I want to push on to new goals, to new contributions. I beg that you save me from the crushing effects of the present circumstances. I must struggle with new vigor, new hope, and new faith—and I need your help.

Oh God I don't know what strange meaning lies in the awful consequences of recent events. I curse the stupid course that my trail has followed. I cannot feel the meaning of it. I am lost. I wander in heavy darkness, not one guiding star in hand, and then I return to reality and to my yearnings for a normal day of work, fatigue, sleep, and the simple pleasures of life.

One must resist so many things when one cannot fight: laziness, unproductiveness, melancholia, despair, loss of strength—mental, physical, and moral. To be held free and yet a prisoner, to have problems and yet not be able to attack them. Oh this, dear God, is the worst cross to bear. Oh, I want to be back in the swing, back in the fight. I want to be spared the endless hours of waiting. I want to be liberated from this banishment, this exile, and I pray, oh God, I pray for guidance, forgiveness.

Give me judgment, coolness, patience, wisdom, courage. Out of this pain, this agony, this despair will come some added knowledge of life, of the world, of myself. But, now, I need the occasion for action, an outlet for energies. I am caught, hemmed in, held back from the things I want to do. I am unhappy but that is unimportant. I want my work, my office, my patients, my life and way of living.

I have fears, yes, and yet I am not wholly afraid. However, I sense how easy it will be for me to coast along, far out at sea and far away from home, family—so many things that I love. I shall dream of them and yearn for them, and they will take on a luster a little beyond their normal brilliance. Perhaps I shall miss them more than I should, but maybe find some escape into some kind of occupation that will live from each corner of my heart.

There is a turning point in the mad stream of time, waves curling and churning around a rock jutting from the shore.

exile
loss of profession
divorce
courts
escape
finances

So what do we search for—pleasure, destiny, fulfillment, love, freedom? We search to right wrongs and to help others, to live a full and complete life. To see one's destiny and not to obey the call is bitter. One must struggle to deserve happiness. One cannot enjoy real happiness without struggling to fulfill the dictates of destiny. We pay the price of pain, of arduous labor, for that which we accomplish. The reward is relief from strain and a sense of accomplishment.

I must become more active. I must struggle harder, more desperately, if not more valiantly. Write, yes, I will write more and more each day. Dreams to be fulfilled, enterprises to complete, ambition to burst into new flame.

One of the goals I seek is to learn to write in a style readable, clear and captivating. I must learn to write and then find out that which I want to express, the stories or books I want to write, the characters to bring to life, which spiritual and intellectual forces to compel into action.

The trail to follow will be long and rough, narrow and winding, vertiginous, as has been the trail that lies behind. You see, luck gave out for a while, just for a few minutes, back in the winter of 1944 and that short luckless period gave my heart many burdens to carry for the rest of my life. I do not read the future, I cannot, but I must guess as best I can and be guided by the dictation of forces and facts.

Somehow I cling to a feeling of confidence in the belief that my own personal destiny has some strange meaning beyond that which I can see in the past or predict for the future. This faint confidence keeps alive within my heart a desire to live, and the desire fights off another yearning: to die, to escape from a world that holds me as a slave, a servant, a prisoner.

I believe in destiny and I believe that fortune and misfortune can be a part of some great plan by which we live and die. Only a few short months ago, I felt triumphant entering a phase of unusual success, triumph, happiness, and then suddenly came a vortex of disasters, suffering, frustration beyond almost anything conceivable, the horrible debacle of being picked up by the police at The Country Club, that painful memory.

A great mass of dark memories collect and whirl around madly, surrounding and engulfing consciousness. The revocation of license, every item and angle of The Country Club scene, every bit of disgrace, magnified and caught in the most intolerable slide, viewed through the high power of a microscope.

Dr. and Mrs. Frothingham, my friends looking on. Around the corner to the police. Helen Webster, my head on her shoulder. We walk together to the bar. She kisses me. "All of Perry's problems are sexual." Handcuffs applied to my hands as I held them behind my back. Three plain-clothes policemen. Three state troopers.

I run in circles. I sit at Mr. and Mrs. Frothingham's table: "They've come to take me to Westborough."

Seen in the hallway, various friends talking with the officers, talking lengthily.

I move down the corridor and into the main living room and there I find Helen.

Seated on the back seat between two state troopers, my hands manacled behind me, two state troopers on the front seat, a long drive to Westborough. I smoke several cigarettes, talk very little. I am caught in a trance. I am shocked beyond sensation.

And so the story unravels itself. A story predestined to take the course it has followed, a character on the stage of life, seemingly driven along by strange compulsions beyond his understanding. So much happened so quickly, so much to remember forever, so much to haunt the corridors of memory. Life moves along strange paths. We are only to such a limited degree the pilot of our soul, the captain of our ship.

PART II

ECHOES DOWN

THE YEARS

My own memories of the day my father was taken away to Westborough are scant. I was not quite six years old—my younger sister Catherine was four. From my small child's perspective, it was a day much like any other. After visiting my father at the Ritz and The Country Club, we came home for dinner. My mother made no mention of what had happened that afternoon. The next morning, my sister and I got up, we got dressed, we had our breakfast, we left for school, and continued on with our daily routines.

In the days to come, it took me a while to notice that my
father had been gone from our home for a longer period than
usual. I was accustomed to his absences—he was a doctor, and
my mother always informed me that doctors worked long hours.
He was a bear of a man, with square shoulders, reddish blond
hair, and vivid brown eyes. My father exuded charisma—the
walls of our house never seemed large enough to contain him. I
longed for his homecomings.

My mother, my sister, and me in the Boston
Public Garden, March 1944, a month after my
father entered Westborough State Hospital.

My mother was a slender, dark-haired woman who moved about our home with nervous determination and rarely stopped to fully listen. When I finally asked her where my father might be, she paused.

"Oh. He's away," she told me, waving her hand in the air dismissively.

In the weeks and months that followed, my mother maintained her silence on the subject. My father was simply "away." Each time I questioned her, she would perform the same routine, waving her hand, as if he had simply disappeared into the wide blue yonder. I had no idea he was being held in a mental institution. I didn't know that she had filed for divorce. Her evasion was deliberate but, I think, well meaning. She was of the generation of parents who never spoke to their children about difficult subjects. My father's "trouble" would have been considered an adult matter, inappropriate for my small child's ears.

After the school year ended in June, we went, as we always did, to Center Lovell, Maine, where my mother's aunt kept a summer home on the shores of Kezar Lake. Here we stayed for the remainder of the summer, joined by an extended family of aunts and cousins. We were in Maine on July 8, when my father escaped from Westborough State Hospital.

By that summer, my father had been gone from my life for half a year. I was old enough to begin questioning everything, to want to put the world's puzzle pieces in order, but I was given very little information with which to construct any type of a picture. My mother continued to tell me that my father was simply "away," an explanation that cruelly left open the possibility of his return. I continued to wait. Every weekend, when the fathers of my playmates came up from the city, I would hope that, perhaps the following weekend, mine would finally appear.

We returned to Chestnut Hill in time for the start of the school year. My school report from September indicates that I was struggling: "In most of her school life, Mimi seems very happy. Any new situation, however, upsets her. The first few days of lunch and the first time the nurse examined her, she burst into tears."

On March 9, 1945, I turned seven years old. My mother organized a small party for me at our home, and eight friends came, all of us decked out in our Sunday best. Our living room was festooned with St. Patrick's Day decorations. We went over to the neighboring farm to see the animals, returning back to the house for pin-the-bone-in-the-dog's-mouth. Much later, I learned from my father's medical records that, the same week, he returned to Boston from Dallas, broke into our garage, stole our car, and tore his police cell to pieces.

It is to my mother's credit that our childhood routine remained as evenly regimented as ever. The days revolved around school, sports, and friends. I remember barely a ripple in the calm pool of our lives, until the following year of 1946. That spring, a new man entered my mother's life. He was a Bostonian executive in a family-owned oil business. Initially, I was welcoming. He was attentive to my sister and me, and my mother's mood improved in his presence. That summer, when he joined us for weekends on vacation in Maine, I was happy enough to see him, though too busy with my usual activities to notice that his relationship with my mother was becoming serious.

Their wedding took place on October 4, 1946. It was a small service attended by seven friends and family members; my sister and I were the flower girls. I was eight years old. I have only a slight memory of this occasion, although the scratchy taffeta of my dress and the smell of gardenias still linger. That same fall, after the honeymoon, we left our home we had shared with our father on Clovelly Road, and moved to a house on nearby Woodland Road.

I grew quietly furious. A family friend once described my new stepfather as a "bantam rooster." It was true that, while he was rather short of stature, he strutted about our house with the clear intention of ruling the roost. I resisted any interaction with him, refusing to comply with his smallest request. Every night, before I went to sleep, my mother would demand that I say good night to him. I never wanted to do it, and so I'd stomp downstairs and stand in the doorway of the living room, before muttering "'night" as I turned to race back upstairs. My mother's remarriage ignited a deeply felt loyalty within me. Although I had only lived with my father for the first six years of my life, I had developed a closeness to him that endured. I was still awaiting his return.

My stepfather, it turned out, was a severe and unfriendly man. He owned many dogs, and when he became upset with me, he would address me as he did his dogs: "Mind!" He disliked reminders of my mother's prior marriage, and so any discussion or mention of my father was frowned upon—the expectation was that we were all to behave as if he had never existed. Looking back, I can see that my mother was in love, and that in my stepfather she had at least found the security she had lacked in her marriage to my father. But at the time, as my school report from that year indicates, all was not well with me:

December 13, 1946—Mimi has had a great deal on her mind this year. She is going through a period of adjustment that is very trying. Confusion and worry are evident. The most obvious result is a very short attention span. She has difficulty concentrating on any of the academics for any length of time.

She does much better in group situations where several children are working on one focal point. Even at times when she is receiving completely individual help, she soon becomes preoccupied with her own thoughts. Since Mimi has shown no drive for better achievement, it does make it difficult to accomplish much. Her whole adjustment is going to take time.

I continued to ask my mother about my father. I kept repeating the question "Why?" Finally, she informed me that my father was "ill." The words "manic-depressive psychosis" were used. I had no idea what this meant, and my mother refused to explain.

. . .

After my mother remarried, it was as if I had lost both of my parents. My stepfather was very possessive of my mother and she was eager to please him. They were often away from the house, at social or business events. Each February they left for the Caribbean, fleeing the New England winter in the hope it would alleviate my stepfather's asthma. My sister and I always stayed behind. On Valentine's Day and Easter, a card appeared, written by our mother before her departure, inscribed with a single word: "Mother."

One year, my mother and stepfather were coming back from their winter trip. Our housekeeper's husband, who worked for us as a driver, picked them up from the airport. On the way home, he warned my mother that she shouldn't expect a warm welcome from me. "Miss Mimi is no longer the cheerful little girl she used to be," he explained. "She has turned into an ice princess." My mother later repeated this exchange to me, emphasizing that this had been the moment she "gave up on me."

In June 1948, I graduated from my elementary school and entered Beaver Country Day School. My teachers soon observed that I was having trouble listening and paying attention. Our principal believed that any student who misbehaved or had marginal grades should consult a child psychologist. On several occasions I was sent to such a doctor in the hope that this would improve my performance at school. The first psychologist had his offices in an old brownstone on Beacon Street in Boston. I went to him twice, during which time I sat in my chair, refusing to say anything. I remember feeling rather proud of this accomplishment. The next psychologist I visited worked at a hospital. Again, I remained mute throughout the session, and again the visits were soon discontinued.

Silence continued to prevail all around me. While I was growing up, many of my father's friends—including some of the doctors treating him for his illness—lived nearby. Their children were my friends and I often spent time at their houses, but I don't remember anyone ever mentioning my father. Out of respect for my mother and in accordance with the social codes of the times, no one breathed a word.

· · ·

One day, five years after my mother remarried, in May 1951, she made a startling announcement at the breakfast table.

"Your father is coming to visit you this afternoon."

I struggled to absorb the meaning of her words. By now I was thirteen. I hadn't seen him in nearly seven years.

"I'll call your school later this afternoon," my mother went on, "and they will send you home to see your father."

I nodded silently. I hoped I would recognize him. Although I had strong memories of his presence in my life, I hadn't seen him in such a long time, and had no photographs of him.

After breakfast, I walked the short distance to school. I went to my morning classes, waiting with apprehension for the afternoon to arrive. As promised, I was summoned to leave and told to go directly home. It was a bright spring day, and I carried my coat, wearing my neat plaid skirt with a white blouse and navy cable-stitched sweater. I followed the school driveway, walking past thick woods to my left, tennis courts to my right. Perhaps I should have raced home in anticipation of a joyful reunion with my father, but instead, I was overcome by an inexplicable feeling of reluctance. The hesitancy was so powerful that, about halfway along the driveway, it stopped me in my tracks. I considered turning back, but I knew my teachers would only send me home again, so I forced myself to keep walking.

A few minutes later, I arrived at my house. I hung up my coat in the closet and immediately ran upstairs to my room, throwing my books on the bed. I turned around and went to the window across the hall from my room and waited, looking down at the road. After a short time, a man in a suit and hat walked up to the front door. The doorbell rang, and my mother called my name.

I went downstairs and into the living room. The man in the suit was sitting next to my mother and stepfather in front of the fireplace. He had removed his hat and I could see he had brownish hair, slicked to the side in the typical style of the times. The suit was dark-colored and hung somewhat loosely on his tall, broad-shouldered frame. I felt a tug of recognition. This was my father.

I don't remember exactly how I greeted him. I doubt that we embraced—it's more likely that we simply stared at one another. What I do know is that at some point, I left to go back to my bedroom and my father followed me. Upstairs, I proudly showed him my room. The house had once belonged to a cardiologist, and my bedroom was in his former library. I showed my father my beloved balcony, my refuge, where I could look down on the terrace at the back of the house. I showed him the letters I kept Scotch-taped to the back of my closet door, including some from my uncle Philip—his brother—in Texas.

We sat on my bed and talked. The exact content of our conversation has faded with the years, but I can still remember how extraordinary it felt to have him there beside me. I knew he didn't belong in this house, and yet at the same time he was so completely familiar to me. Soon he got up to go, quietly descending the stairway. I listened as the front door closed.

The day after his visit, I was upstairs in my room doing my homework. I heard voices, some kind of commotion downstairs. I went to the hallway window. Looking down, I could see my father. He was stumbling along the front walk that led to the street, wearing yesterday's dark suit. Today it was rumpled. He walked to the curb and sat down. I watched him for some time. He seemed very different from the previous day: his shoulders were slumped, his hat was off, and his head was in his hands. If I had been more experienced, perhaps I would have recognized that he was inebriated, but I had no context for his behavior. After a while, I stepped away from the window. When I looked once more he had gone. I never saw him again. Nonetheless, our time in my room and even that brief sighting of him outside the window reinforced my connection to him, a feeling that I carry with me to this day.

• • •

As the years went on, the question of my father's absence continued, insistent and unanswered. I ignored its refrain as best I could, trying hard to maintain my mother's code of silence. These were the 1950s. You did not whine. You did not complain. "You're made of sterner stuff" were the watchwords of every parent and teacher at that time. When any feeling of confusion about my father surfaced, I pushed it away, forcing my mind to go blank. The blankness came at a cost, and I was in a permanent state of distraction during my teenage years. I found it especially challenging to pay attention and to retain information, and there are tremendous holes in my education as a result. There are holes in the emotional fabric of my life, too.

In 1953, my mother and stepfather decided that I might do better at boarding school, so I was sent to a school in Middlebury, Connecticut. I was eighteen and in my senior year when my father sent me the only letter I ever received from him. It was delivered to our Chestnut Hill address, and my mother, without opening the letter, forwarded it to me at school. I opened it immediately. Inside, I found a photograph of Elaine Stewart, a popular, rather voluptuous actress of that time. A note was attached from my father indicating that she looked quite like me. I knew the tone and content of the letter were inappropriate. I tore up the photograph and note and threw them away, dismayed. My roommate found me not long afterwards, curled inside my closet, weeping.

. . .

Three years later I graduated from Colby-Sawyer College. I went to work in Cambridge as a secretary at the dean's office of the Harvard Graduate School of Education. This was a happy time for me—I enjoyed my job and newfound independence, sharing an apartment on Marlborough Street with three girlfriends. Various friends were beginning to pair off and get married, and I knew that soon I would do the same. There was a feeling for all of us that life was just beginning.

Then, in May 1959, a year after my college graduation, I received a telephone call from my mother.

"Your father has died," she informed me, without preamble. "You are to travel to Texas for the funeral right away."

Stunned by her announcement, I did as I was told. I hung up the telephone and began my preparations, grabbing clothing from hangers and packing various items in my suitcase. I sensed that this activity would be easier than trying to comprehend the loss of a father I had always missed—but who now was truly gone—and whose funeral I had just been inexplicably commanded to attend.

The following day, my sister, who was still in college, met me at Logan Airport and we flew to Dallas together. We spent the duration of the flight in uncomprehending silence. My mother's aunt, our great-aunt Martha, who lived in Dallas, met us at the airport and took us to her apartment. The next morning, we drove to church to attend our father's funeral.

His obituary appeared that week in the local newspaper, although I didn't see it until many years later:

Dr. Perry C. Baird Funeral Rites Slated Thursday

Funeral services for Dr. Perry Cossart Baird Jr., 55, a Dallas native and at one time an internationally known dermatologist, will be held at 11:30 a.m. Thursday.

Dr. Baird died Monday in a Detroit, Mich. hotel. He moved to Detroit six weeks ago to enter business.

He attended Dallas public schools and Southern Methodist University, and graduated from the University of Texas with honors, including Phi Beta Kappa. He later attended Harvard Medical School, graduating with the highest honors ever awarded a graduate at that time.

In addition to his private practice he served on the staff of Peter Bent Brigham Hospital in Boston, Mass., and as dermatologist consultant and teacher at Harvard. He lived in Boston about 20 years. Persons throughout the world consulted him during his years in Boston.

Dr. Baird returned to Dallas about 10 years ago after his retirement. He was a member of numerous service and private clubs in Boston.

Survivors are two daughters, Miss Mimi Baird and Miss Catherine Baird, both of Boston, Mass.; two brothers, James G. Baird of Minden, La., and Lewis P. Baird of Dallas; one sister, Mrs. W. O. Williamson Jr. of Atlanta, Ga.; and his mother, Mrs. Perry C. Baird of Dallas.

The funeral service was held at a small chapel, but I have few other memories of our two days in Dallas, except that, despite the sad occasion, our Texan relatives were overjoyed to see us. We had been estranged from our father's family since the divorce fifteen years ago and over the next few days, we spent our time continually being introduced to relatives that we didn't know. Despite our bewilderment, my grandparents and aunts and uncles treated us with unguarded love and enthusiasm. Everywhere we went people gathered around us and photographs were taken.

By then, my grandmother—who was known to all as Momma B.—was frail and elderly, but she was particularly delighted to see us, repeatedly wrapping us in hugs. The reunion evidently meant a great deal to her, and I wish I'd had the maturity at the time to understand the reason. Perry had been her dearest son, and the appearance of her long-lost granddaughters at his funeral must have been a source of much consolation. This could have been the beginning of a new relationship with our grandmother, but in fact, it was the last time we saw her. Three months after my father's passing, she followed him, dying brokenhearted.

CHAPTER SIXTEEN

After the funeral, my sister and I flew back to Boston. The following day, I returned to my usual routine, and my sister resumed her studies. In the ensuing weeks, I put away the confusing matter of our father's death, diverting my attentions to my job and social life.

Soon after, I became engaged. It was 1960, and my ambitions were those of so many young women at that time: I wanted to be a wife; I wanted to have a family.

A few weeks before my wedding day, my mother took me to one side.

"You don't need to worry," she informed me. "Your father's trouble can't be inherited. Your children will be fine."

I stared at her in disbelief. It had never occurred to me that my father's illness might be inherited. I had no understanding of manic depression—it had never been talked about or adequately explained to me. I certainly never thought to look it up in a medical dictionary; the subject was completely taboo.

"Thank you, mother," I responded. End of conversation.

After my son and my daughter were born, in 1961 and 1963, I put my focus squarely on my children. I absorbed myself in their daily development, delighting in the milestones along the way. It was only when I emerged from their early childhood years that the mystery of my father began to trouble me again. I knew I had been given incomplete information about my family history and therefore, on some level, I felt myself to be incomplete. What had taken place all those years ago in the house on Clovelly Road? Where had my father gone and why had we never visited him? Surely my mother wouldn't deny me some basic information at this point. I was an adult now, with children of my own.

But it wasn't until the fall of 1969 that I got up the courage to call her, letting her know that I had things on my mind and that I wanted to visit to talk about my father. I made a special trip to Woodstock, Vermont, to the country home she shared with my stepfather. My mother was in her late fifties by then, and strands of gray were starting to appear in her hair, but she still found it hard to sit and listen, preferring to be in constant, nervous motion. The afternoon of my arrival, we went to sit in the outdoor porch, with its beautiful views of Mount Ascutney. The autumn air was chilled.

"Mother, I would like to ask you some questions about my father."

Instinctively she looked around at the screen door that led to the living room, trying to ascertain if my stepfather was within earshot.

"What happened after he left us?"

"Your father was ill," she replied, using those same words she had always rolled out. "He had manic-depressive psychosis."

"I know. But didn't you ever visit him? Where was he?"

"Your father was . . . hard to see," she replied, slowly.

I could see my stepfather peering through the screen door to the porch, straining his neck for a better view. My mother was shuffling in her seat, as if she couldn't wait for the interrogation to be over.

"What did his doctors say about him?" I asked.

"Really," she said impatiently. "I don't remember."

Meanwhile, my stepfather appeared on the opposite side of the porch, beginning—rather unconvincingly—to rearrange the wood stacks piled up near the outdoor fireplace. I marveled at his determination to interrupt our conversation; nonetheless, I was resolved to continue.

"Mother, did you ever consider taking me to see him?"

"Maybe I did," she replied. "It was so long ago. I don't know how you expect me to remember."

"I think it's only fair that I should know."

My stepfather turned around from the other side of the porch.

"Gretta," he called, "it's growing cold out here. I think you should come inside."

That was the end of it. My mother went inside and the conversation was closed.

．．．

My mother's reticence wasn't only due to stubbornness; in fact, it had deep roots in her own childhood. Not only had she married a man with manic depression, my mother had been born to a father with the exact same illness.

I must have been in high school when she happened to mention, in her offhand way, that her father, Henry Gibbons, had also suffered with manic depression.

"I was ten years old when he went away," she told me. "He spent the rest of his life in a hospital in Norristown, Pennsylvania."

Growing up, I had always been informed that my grandfather was deceased and that my grandmother was a widow. No one spoke of him. The family simply behaved as if he didn't exist. Only later did I learn from my mother that—for most of my childhood—my grandfather Henry had been very much alive and locked away in a psychiatric institution.

In other words, my mother and I had an extraordinary bond, however unspoken. We had both lost our fathers to mental illness. This might have brought us closer together. Instead, the opposite was true. My mother's refusal to talk about what had happened to my father was a direct echo of the events of her own childhood. Her father, Henry, had been hidden away; therefore my father's circumstances must also be hidden. This was simply the way things were done. Silence was an inheritance.

. . .

Even so, as the years went on, I still held out hope that I would be able to open the lines of communication with my mother. Every now and again, I would make another overture, to no avail. My sister, meanwhile, followed my mother's lead. Catherine had little interest in talking about the past. She had been a toddler when our father was taken away. As far as she was concerned, he had simply never featured in her life, and that was that.

It was different for me. I could remember being with my father at his doctor's offices on Commonwealth Avenue, the familiar scent of sterile instruments in the air. I could recall him proudly taking a photograph of me wearing a cowgirl outfit that my grandmother had given me for my birthday. In another memory, I could remember looking for my father, going upstairs to the little bathroom adjacent to my parents' bedroom to find him stepping out of the shower, wrapping a towel around his middle. To me, he seemed as tall as the giants

in my fairytale book. My memories of my father's presence came
back to me in bright flashes.

· · ·

After my stepfather passed away, and the Woodstock summer
house was sold, I moved to that same Vermont village, a place
I had always loved. It was 1979. My children were teenagers,
and I had decided to return to work. I applied for a job at the
prominent teaching hospital across the Connecticut River in
New Hampshire, where I started in an entry-level secretarial
job. Some months later, I was hired as the office manager in the
department of plastic surgery.

During the move to Vermont, as I packed up my possessions,

I came across a box of my father's belongings that my mother had given me when I went to college. These included some of his old books, photograph albums, and other mementoes, including two silver Paul Revere bowls my father had inscribed to celebrate his riding victories and a gold pin he had given my mother as a present. In the same box were two tin canisters of home movies marked "Perry/Gretta wedding, 1931." With the holidays approaching, I decided to have the old film converted to VCR format, so I could give my mother the video for Christmas. I assumed the wedding film would be a nice surprise for her and might prompt some much-needed discussion between us.

Before I put the videotape in the mail, I sat in my living room to watch it. The grainy, black-and-white footage clearly showed my father and mother on their wedding day. They were standing next to one another in the receiving line against a dark background, from which their figures seemed to emerge like ghosts. My girlish mother was giddy with love and excitement. My father was tall and proud, if a little dazed. Toward the end of the video, my father bent down to give my mother a long, lingering kiss. I caught my breath. Later that day, I put the tape in a box and mailed it to my mother with great anticipation. I told my family members who would be with her on Christmas day not to reveal the contents of the tape until it began to play in the video machine.

I learned later that when my mother realized it was her wedding footage, she got up and left the room. No further mention of the tape was ever made. After this episode, I resolved never to bring up my father's name in my mother's presence again.

. . .

It was another ten years before I heard anyone speak of him. I continued my work at the hospital, surrounded by doctors and nurses each day, feeling a great sense of purpose in my job and appreciation for the medical environment. Then, one bright fall day in October 1991, I was scheduled to attend an opening event at our new hospital building. We had just moved in and were celebrating.

The day of the reception, I was in good spirits. I'd been out of the office for a few weeks, and so spent most of that afternoon catching up with my colleagues on the latest news from around the department. Later, I went over to speak to the guest of honor, a pioneering plastic surgeon named Dr. Radford Tanzer, after whom our new space was being named. I had worked with Dr. Tanzer for a time and had always admired him. He was now in his mid-eighties, and had the same compassionate and intelligent eyes that must have reassured many generations of patients.

During the course of our brief conversation, I mentioned to Dr. Tanzer that my father had been a doctor.

"What was your father's name?" the surgeon asked.

"Perry Baird," I replied.

Dr. Tanzer looked at me and paused.

"I knew your father," he said quietly. "We were at Harvard Medical School together."

The noise of the party seemed to ebb away in the wake of his words.

"I graduated the year after him, in 1929," Dr. Tanzer went on. "We both attended lectures at the St. Botolph's Club in Boston."

It was the first time in my life *anyone* had spoken to me about my father in this way, as if he were an actual person, someone who went to Harvard, attended lectures at a club, and who *knew* people. Moments later, Dr. Tanzer was led away to speak with another party guest. I wasn't able to ask him for any more information. Nonetheless, the effect of this short exchange on my life was profound: it validated my feeling that something significant was missing from my understanding of my early years.

The following Monday, I told another surgeon at the hospital, Dr. Morain, about the extraordinary coincidence. Dr. Morain asked me some questions, and I shared with him the very little I knew. Although my mother had always been more or less mute on the subject of her first husband, she had once told me that Dr. Walter B. Cannon was one of my father's mentors. Dr. Morain responded that Dr. Cannon was one of the most important physiologists of the twentieth century.

A week later, Dr. Morain walked into my office, proudly holding a large manila envelope in his hands. He explained that he had been in Boston that weekend for a meeting and had decided to look in Harvard Medical School's Countway Library of Medicine for any trace of my father. In the Walter B. Cannon archive, he had found a cache of my father's letters to Dr. Cannon and copies of Dr. Cannon's replies. Incredibly, the elderly lady librarian—about to retire—remembered my father and refused to charge for copying the file. I thanked Dr. Morain profusely.

Later that evening, I sat leafing through the many dozens of pages inside the envelope. Most of the correspondence was typewritten, but some of the letters were in my father's handwriting, a large looping script. As I flipped from page to page, my eyes froze at one of the letterheads: 32 Clovelly Road, Chestnut Hill—the little white clapboard where I'd lived with my father and mother all those years ago.

I imagined my father sitting there at his writing desk in the house, the promising young doctor corresponding with one of the most famous physicians of the times. The earliest letters were written in 1928, during the period when my father had been a research assistant to Dr. Cannon. The two men discussed my father's career, the appointments he should seek, and how he should move forward with his work.

Throughout the letters, I found repeated mention of Dr. James Howard Means, Chief of Medical Services at Massachusetts General Hospital. So I decided to visit Harvard's Countway Library to see if Dr. Means's archive might hold further letters from my father. The library is housed in a modern concrete structure on the outskirts of Boston, and as I walked into its large entry area, I was struck by the quiet solemnity of the place. I placed my request with the librarian and waited, as she disappeared behind two large wooden doors. Before long, she returned with a large folder of correspondence between my father and Dr. Means. I sat at one of the long wooden tables, alongside students and researchers, running my eyes across page after page. The letters spanned the early 1920s to the late 1940s. As far as I could ascertain, Dr. Means's tone was very similar to that of Dr. Cannon: warm, friendly, and encouraging to his younger protégé.

"A man of the finest type of character," Dr. Means wrote of my father in a letter of recommendation from 1933, "upright and sincere in every way, unselfish, brilliant and delightful, very loyal to his friends and principles. His integrity is beyond question. There is no doubt whatever but that Dr. Baird is an internist of superior ability."

As I read, shadows from the afternoon light rippled across the pages. My father's story was emerging from the silence.

CHAPTER SEVENTEEN

The discovery of the letters emboldened me. Some months after that, I was scheduled to attend a plastic surgery conference in Dallas, Texas, for my work. I decided that while I was there, I would look up my uncle Philip, my father's brother. I had no information as to his whereabouts except that he lived in Dallas. As soon as I arrived at my hotel, I opened up the telephone book and looked for his name, fearing I would lose my nerve if I didn't call right away. There were three Philip Bairds listed. I quickly dialed one of the numbers. A woman answered. No, she had never heard of me. I dialed the second number. A man who evidently was not my uncle answered and I hung up quickly. I was about to give up, but instead decided to try the last number.

"Hello," came the voice from the other end of the line. A slow Texas "hello" with the "o" drawn out. I recognized his tone immediately.

"Hello, this is Mimi Baird," I announced.

My uncle's response was immediate: "Why didn't you write back?"

I felt a pang of shame. When I was a child, Uncle Philip had written me a number of letters. I had taped them to the inside of my closet door, the secret place where I stored my treasures. They were extremely precious to me, as one of my only connections to my father. I'd just never known how to respond, and so they had always gone unanswered. My uncle had been waiting for a reply for over forty years.

I told him, truthfully, that I didn't know why, I just never felt able to write.

"I was so young," I told him. "I wish I had."

We agreed to meet the next day.

Philip came to my hotel. As I waited for him in the foyer, I tried to picture him. We must have met at my father's funeral, but I couldn't recall his face. Would he look like my father? After a few minutes, an older man, rather disheveled, wearing white baggy shorts and a faded blue sports shirt, appeared on the other side of the lobby. In the back of my mind I remembered that Uncle Philip had played tennis. I stood up and walked toward him.

"Uncle Philip?" I asked.

He immediately enfolded me in a hug.

We went to take a seat in the little café next to the lobby. Philip sat down. It was clear he was uninterested in polite chitchat.

"Your mother neglected her responsibilities as a wife," he told me, his face folding into a frown. "She deserted your father."

Despite my own reservations about my mother's actions, I felt myself wanting to leap to her defense. I knew that my great-aunt Martha had contributed a considerable amount of money for my father to stay in a private mental institution. I offered this information to Philip, noting that my mother had two young children to think about.

"We were the ones who had to pick up the pieces after your mother divorced him," he responded sternly. "Everything fell to us."

Philip explained that he and his wife—along with my

father's elderly parents—shouldered the burden of caring for my father.

"Your father had a lobotomy," Philip told me. "After that, he could barely tie his own shoelaces. We had to do everything for him. Brush his teeth, buckle his belt. He was never the same."

I remembered hearing the adults around me speaking about lobotomy once, but I had had no idea what they'd meant.

Philip told me that after the surgery, my father was given medication to help with his recovery—but too much medication made him dizzy. When he forgot to take his pills, he would have seizures.

"Even after the lobotomy, he still got into trouble," Philip remembered, "especially if he drank. I'd be called out to rescue him from barroom fights or from the police station."

I sensed that, just as my uncle had been waiting for me to reply to his letters, he had been waiting to tell me my father's story.

"Maybe there's still some way I can make amends," I said, rather helplessly.

Soon, he got up to leave. After we hugged goodbye, he offered me one last piece of information.

"Your father was writing a book," he said, scrawling a number on a paper napkin.

"It's your cousin's number," he explained. "My son Randy. He has the manuscript. Call him."

I walked Philip out to his car and watched him drive away, holding my cousin's number in my hand.

. . .

Later that evening, after my duties at the conference were completed and I was back in my hotel room, I dialed my cousin Randy's number. He answered and I introduced myself. We'd never met, never as much as spoken, and yet for the duration of the conversation, we chatted easily and warmly, perhaps both trying to make up for lost time. I learned that Randy lived in Austin. Over the next two days, we spoke on the telephone as often as we could, catching up on family matters on both sides. Eventually, I brought up the subject of the manuscript.

Randy confirmed that he had rescued it from his father's house a few years back.

"My father and mother didn't want it. There used to be a typed version, but that disappeared a long time ago."

The manuscript was sitting in an old briefcase in his garage.

The day before I left Dallas, my cousin telephoned to let me know he had spoken with his wife, Karen. They both felt the manuscript belonged with me.

. . .

Several weeks later, I returned home from work to find the large carton on my doorstep with a return address in Austin. I called Texas the next day.

"We're so very happy," Randy's wife, Karen, told me. "At last, they're where they belong. Perry's little girl has his papers. We've only been the caretakers."

The pages of my father's manuscript were completely out of sequence. I did my best to make sense of his words. On one page he was writing about having breakfast at the Ritz. On the next he was being violently restrained by hospital guards.

If these pages held the key to the mystery of my father, they weren't going to give up their secrets easily.

I tried to match them into some kind of order, glancing at each line and looking for key words to group the writing according to subject. Much of the writing was clearly about his confinement in Westborough. I learned to look for the names of the various wards where he had been kept, then evidence of his transfer to Baldpate. I recognized names of old family friends; my mother's name, Gretta, appeared frequently. I became familiar with sequences of events and made piles of paper, according to the names of people, events, and places.

My father's handwriting was another guide. On some pages the script was meticulously placed, with many straight lines on each page. In other instances, his handwriting became large and increasingly irregular, the background covered with dark smudges.

In the coming weeks, I lived with the papers still stacked in their piles around my kitchen as I continued to rearrange them according to a tentative timeline. The process was complicated by the fact that my father often drafted the same passage more than once, in slightly differing versions. I kept working, trying to restore the manuscript to its intended order. I was constantly hunting for clues to help me reassemble the story, never knowing what I might find next.

One day, reading through pages, I saw a word I'd never noticed before.

Mimi.

I read the entire page. My father was writing about staying at the Ritz Hotel. My mother arrived at his room with my sister and me in tow. She wouldn't sit down and got ready to leave almost immediately. Then I spoke:

> *"I want to stay with daddy."*

It wasn't until I saw these words that the events of the manuscript became entirely real to me. I had been there. I had a voice. I had wanted to stay with my father.

. . .

Once the pages were in some kind of order, I began typing up his words. Initially I struggled to decipher his handwriting, but before long, I became familiar with the shape of his b's, his l's, his f's. Just as I became accustomed to the contours of his letters, I also became better at detecting the levels of his sanity. For entire pages, he appeared to be completely in control of his mind. He wrote as a man of science, observing the scene as if he were a doctor visiting the hospital, rather than a patient being held there. His handwriting in these passages was orderly and regular. Then, suddenly, it would become expansive, out of control, when his grip on his sanity was slipping. Then pages and pages of visions and delusions, his script slanting to the right, the handwriting ballooning, as the urgency to get his message down on the page superseded any other concern.

After some weeks of working on the manuscript, I was handling the onionskin pages so much that I feared that they would become damaged. The pages were delicate, and were written on with pencil that smudged easily. I felt it was my great responsibility to protect my father's words. The chances of his manuscript surviving were so slim, and yet it had ended up with my uncle in Dallas, then with my cousin in Austin, and now—so many years later—with me in Vermont. I was the caretaker now.

I purchased a box of clear, acid-free folders. That evening, I sat in my living room, sliding the pages of the manuscript inside the folders, one at a time. I was so absorbed in my task that I didn't notice my fingers becoming blackened by the pencil from the pages. Only when I was finished did I see that my fingertips were darkened with lead.

I turned my palms up and held them before my eyes, transfixed. The thought went through my head: *My father put this lead on these papers, now it has come away on my hands.* The connection I'd always felt between us was tangible.

CHAPTER EIGHTEEN

I t was clear that my father was writing about the events of 1944, the last year I'd lived with him. Emerging before me was the story of what had happened to him during those first months of his absence. Although my father's descriptions of his time in the hospital were horrifying to read, my work was spurred on by a sense of duty. As I typed each sentence, watching the words appear on the computer screen, it was further proof that he had existed.

As I tried to absorb the meaning of his experiences, instinctively, I turned to books for help and guidance. What did it even mean that my father was "manic"? I found a copy of *The Bell Jar* and read Sylvia Plath's novelized account of her breakdown and electric shock treatment. I read psychiatrist Kay Redfield Jamison's *An Unquiet Mind,* about her own experiences of manic depression. I read William Styron's startling memoir of his descent into madness, *Darkness Visible.* Over the next few months, I read as many books on mental illness and manic depression as I could find.

I kept a notebook and created page after page of quotes, looking for clues with which to plot some kind of map. I became a student of the condition, its violent and disruptive mood swings, the intense highs followed by the terrifying lows. I came to understand that, despite the menace of the disorder, manic depression is often closely allied with genius. Many of our greatest artists have been sufferers, "touched with fire," as

Jamison has written of Lord Byron, Vincent van Gogh, Virginia Woolf, and Ernest Hemingway, among many others.

The work progressed slowly. My inclination was to conduct my research a little at a time. The material I was uncovering was so unsettling that after all these years of not knowing, each discovery had to be assimilated slowly, piece by piece.

I found other traces of him, beyond the manuscript. There was the pink cloth-covered baby book where my mother recorded the small milestones of my early years, pages that are filled with references to me with my father. My mother writes that the first time I put words together in a sentence, it was to ask, "Where's Daddy?" At the age of three, it is noted, I'd sit on my father's lap while he read to me his favorite poems from *The Rubáiyát of Omar Khayyám.* Before long, I could quote the first lines back to him: "Awake! For morning in the bowl of night has flung the stone that puts the stars to flight."

Somewhere in my house, I knew, there was a cache of albums containing photographs and letters of his, given to me by my mother. I was a teenager when I'd first inherited them, and I had dismissed them as relics. Now I felt certain they could help me become a better student of my father's life. I eventually located two albums tucked away in the back of one of my bookcases. The first was his baby book, its delicately worn, light blue leather covers embossed with gold. Inside, each page was decorated in the Victorian style, with golden curlicues, and images of flowers and baby faces. I found sepia studio photographs of father as a handsome toddler in overalls, his hair a mass of shining curls. In careful, steady script, my grandmother had noted the date of his first smile, his first steps, his first word. She had even preserved a lock of his baby hair. I tentatively ran my finger over the soft and glossy strands, marveling at their survival.

A second album kept by my grandmother contained my father's school reports and photographs of him as a schoolboy. There were high school newspaper clippings indicating his many academic achievements. One article reported that he was "highly motivated and always looking toward the next goal at top speed." He played football and was elected president of his senior class.

A letter, from 1921, contained news that he had been accepted to the University of Texas. The next letter confirmed that, after only the first semester, he had made the college honor roll. The following year, he wrote home to tell his parents he had been given a coveted assistantship by the chemistry department, and that he wished to take it, to "put me in a better position to be elected to Phi Beta Kapa in the fall." He graduated that year summa cum laude, having completed the university's four-year curriculum in three years. I imagined my grandmother's pride as she received these letters, each one signed, affectionately, "Perry Boy."

The photographs from his time at the University of Texas showed a confident, handsome young man. His hair was light reddish brown, his nose somewhat prominent, and his ears slightly large, but it was the intense determination of his gaze that held my attention. After graduation my father set his sights on Harvard Medical School. When he received his letter of acceptance, he gave it to his mother, who dutifully pasted it in her scrapbook.

HARVARD UNIVERSITY
MEDICAL SCHOOL

DAVID L. EDSALL, M.D.
                    Dean
WORTH HALE, M.D.
                    Assistant Dean   *Boston 17, Massachusetts*

Dear Sir:
            I am glad to say the Committee on Admission has
decided to offer you a place in the Harvard Medical School.
Please let me know by return mail whether or not you can
accept this place.
            The $50. deposit which insures your place must be
mailed before August 1st, and is applied to your first
term bill or forfeited in case you fail to register. After
we receive your deposit we will send you a blank bond and
certain other forms to be filled in. Check should be made
payable to Harvard University and forwarded to me.
            School will open on September 22nd and we shall
be very glad to see you then.

                                    Yours very truly,

            July 16, 1924   *Worth Hale*
                                    Assistant Dean

The senior members of the Harvard Medical School faculty
soon began to take notice of my father's talents. In the summer
of 1927, my father sent a telegram home saying that he had
been invited to join Dr. Walter B. Cannon's Harvard laboratory as a research assistant in physiology for one year. He had
quickly accepted the prestigious offer.

I kept waiting for some indication of my father's mental
troubles. Finally, I found a letter from September of 1927. My
father was writing home after a brief visit to Texas:

> The invariable consequences of quickly changing
> surroundings from a pleasant southern atmosphere
> to the cool, grim, business-like and ultra-progressive
> atmosphere of Boston—is a siege of depression,
> from which one recovers.

Such sieges had little effect on his extraordinary academic
career. By the time he graduated from Harvard in 1928, he had

coauthored five scientific papers that were accepted for publication in the *American Journal of Physiology*. He received his medical degree in 1928, magna cum laude, which was awarded not only for his high academic standing but also for his excellent work on his thesis in physiology. It was the highest academic honor ever awarded up to that time to any Harvard Medical School graduate.

. . .

I continued to keep notes, writing them down on random slips of paper, large and small, yellow lined legal pads, and even on the backs of bank deposit slips, whatever was handy.

In the new year of 1995, I applied for my father's medical records. The process was familiar to me from my job at the hospital, where I was often asked to obtain patient records. The copies of my father's records arrived in the mail in batches. At the end of the application process, I had hundreds of documents, some typed, some handwritten, some in the form of graphs and charts. I could learn what my father had eaten, his temperature, and the quality of his blood and urine work. The records also gave me dates—dates of hospitalizations, dates of release, dates of escapes, dates of treatment—enabling me to put my father's story in context and in order.

Using the medical records as a guide, I went back to my father's letters to Dr. Cannon and Dr. Means, looking for connections. Reading them closely, I learned that my father's medical career was compromised by his illness only three years after his graduation from Harvard. In 1931, the same year he married my mother, he wrote to Dr. Cannon that it was his wish to follow him into the specialty of physiology. Dr. Cannon responded immediately this might prove to be "too stressful" for someone with my father's "sensibilities." Dr. Cannon agreed with Dr. Means that my father would be the ideal man to help spearhead a soon-to-be-revamped department of dermatology at Massachusetts General Hospital. They voted my father a stipend to support his training, and Means arranged for him to interview with the Hospital of the University of Pennsylvania in Philadelphia, where he was quickly offered a position.

My father began his one-year residency in Philadelphia. Not long after, he resumed research work he had initially undertaken at Massachusetts General Hospital under the auspices of Dr. Fuller Albright of the Harvard Medical School faculty. Dr. Albright was one of the guiding lights in the field of endocrinology (the study of diseases relating to the hormones), and my father was invited to coauthor a paper with him on Addison's disease, a disorder of the adrenal glands that caused abnormal pigmentation of the skin.

Again, the rapid advancement of my father's career was stalled by his illness.

Soon after the paper on Addison's Disease was completed, my father had his first severe manic episode and was hospitalized at the Philadelphia Hospital for Mental and Nervous Diseases. After his release, he had to take a two-week break from his work, during which time he became profoundly depressed. His medical records state: "He slept on an average of fourteen hours a day. It was at this time that he was told that, because of the manic episode, he could not be appointed Professor of Dermatology at Harvard." It was a devastating blow.

His mentors raised the idea that he should go into private practice, to better suit his unpredictable mental state. In late

June of 1933, my father wrote to Dr. Means that he was considering an offer from Drs. Lane and Greenwood, dermatologists in Boston. He stressed that he felt "thoroughly rested and perfectly fit for a long period of good hard work." Days later, he accepted the offer and my parents moved to Boston.

• • •

I interviewed family friends who had known my father during his Boston years. I first visited Dr. Marshall Bartlett and his wife, Barbara, at their retirement community in Westwood, just outside the city. Dr. Bartlett had been at Harvard Medical School with my father, had even been present the night my parents first met. He had remained a close family friend ever since. The Bartletts were elderly, but much as I remembered them—Dr. Bartlett had the same distinguished features of his younger years, and Mrs. Bartlett was as gracious as ever.

I told them that I hoped to learn more about my father's professional life.

Dr. Bartlett informed me that although my father had started out at the offices of Lane and Greenwood, he was soon overbooked and ready to open his own practice.

"Word got around through other doctors that 'the best person to go to is Dr. Baird,'" Barbara added.

"I went to him as a patient," Dr. Bartlett told me. "I thought he was the best in town."

Socially, my father was equally successful. The Bartletts remembered him at that time as charismatic and attractive, always at the center of attention, drink in his hand, sometimes playing the piano. No one among my father's social set identified him as having a mental problem in those early days.

"We all thought he had this giant personality," Dr. Bartlett told me. "He didn't hide the fact he was a Texan, a bit of a wild man. He enjoyed his reputation—he could get a little crazy, but people loved him for it. Your father once rented a whole floor of the Copley Plaza for a party—that was the talk of the town."

"When did the problems begin?"

"The first time I noticed he was becoming unstable was after we'd had a conversation about cars," Dr. Bartlett recalled. "Cadillac had just come out with the LaSalle. The next thing I knew, your father had bought two. His moods began to change. You never knew when you went to see him if you were going to get the old Perry or the difficult one."

After leaving the Bartletts, I drove to Chestnut Hill to visit with two of our old neighbors. Frank Shaw still lived two doors down from the house I had shared with my mother and step-father. His house was so familiar to me—with its dark brown clapboards and thick metal separating the windowpanes, it had the austere aura of a church rectory.

Mr. Shaw was tall, confident, and friendly. He reminded me that he had been one of my father's riding partners. The success of my father's practice allowed him to indulge in one of his favorite sports, riding. He purchased three horses: Viking, Sea Gull, and Country Boy. They were kept at Powers Stable, in Dover, not far from our home.

"We lived like kings in those days," Frank recalled rather wistfully. "Tuesdays, Thursdays, and Saturdays, we'd get up at five for morning hunts. Then we'd be at our offices in Boston by 9:30 a.m. for a day's work. Perry always had lunch at the Ritz."

"He never relaxed," Shaw remembered. "He was super-charged with energy. He wasn't a good ride, in the sense of hands and skill, but when he got in the saddle, he stayed in the saddle. He wanted to beat everyone—other riders didn't care for him, but he was a great athlete."

"One day, your father and mother, myself, and my wife, together with another couple, went for a picnic beside Mount Chocorua," Shaw went on, referring to a summit in the White Mountains of New Hampshire. "It was very pleasant, leaves in full colors. I brought along some wine and we had a picnic. Then the rest of us started to walk up the mountain. But Perry didn't walk up anything. He ran up that mountain, full tilt."

Only as the afternoon wore on did Mr. Shaw drift closer to the subject of my father's illness.

"He went to the Ritz whenever he felt himself becoming manic," Mr. Shaw recalled. "He'd stay there drinking large amounts of Coca-Cola, sometimes alcohol. I learned to steer clear when he got in that state."

That was as far as Mr. Shaw seemed to wish to venture. I didn't press further. I thanked him and we said our goodbyes.

Finally I drove to the nearby home of Mrs. Virginia Fenno, another riding partner of my father's. She had been our neighbor then and still lived next door to the house on Clovelly Road. Mrs. Fenno was an elegant-looking woman, tall, with excellent posture, not a hair out of place. She asked after my mother and my children, and I told her that all was well, and that I hoped to learn more about my father.

"Your father was an exceptional man," Mrs. Fenno observed. "He was very competitive and hated to lose. We had a friend, Maynard Johnson, who was much bigger than him. Maynard had rowed for Harvard and was strong as an ox. Your father kept challenging him to a wrestling match. One night, they were at a party and Maynard finally agreed. They wrestled to an absolute draw. It wouldn't have ended but the other doctors pulled them apart."

She also recalled the times she spent riding with my father.

"I always rode with a group of doctors every Sunday morning. Your father was one of them. Then we'd stop and have drinks at someone's house. After Pearl Harbor, all the doctors went away, serving overseas. Your father was very disappointed. He so wanted to go. We still rode once a week. He seemed very depressed at the time. He would often talk about how a 'friend' of his was very depressed and how difficult it was. I felt sure he was speaking about himself.

"The second year of the war, he was becoming more manic. He had this big crush on a friend of mine. He was always trying to persuade her to ride with him. One time, when all of us were out riding together, he convinced her to ride on ahead with him. I stayed back with her husband. Finally her husband, who was a poor ride, said, 'Don't you think you should catch them? Please see what is going on.' I did. Perry was furious. He got his horse excited. We raced up the hill. I realized I couldn't stop my horse. I rode deliberately for the bushes and the horse stopped dead. I was thrown but not hurt. I never rode with Perry again."

The afternoon light was fading and I sensed it was time for me to go. Before I left, I thanked Mrs. Fenno for her time. She took my hand.

"Your father, he couldn't help himself. You know, Mimi, he wanted the moon."

CHAPTER NINETEEN

As I continued to study the letters and medical records, another startling facet of my father's story revealed itself. Not only was he suffering from manic depression. He had been studying it, too.

In 1933, while my father was establishing his dermatology practice in Boston, Dr. Cannon wrote to inform him that space in his laboratory at Massachusetts General had become available. Dr. Cannon was now able to offer my father a minor appointment as a graduate assistant in research. My father didn't hesitate to accept. Despite the interruption of his breakdown, his article on Addison's disease had been accepted for publication in the *American Journal of Physiology* and he was buoyed up by its success. Together with Dr. Albright, he had proven that patients with Addison's disease were deficient in cortin, a natural hormone secreted by the body's adrenal glands. This discovery would later contribute to the development of the steroid cortisone.

It was time for him to find a new research subject, and he knew exactly where his interests lay. Only a few months earlier, he had experienced his first stay in a mental institution, in Philadelphia. Here he had been held in straightjackets and subjected to a week and a half of narcosis "sleep therapy." He felt certain there had to be a more sophisticated approach to the treatment of manic depression. Could there be a connection between the adrenal glands and his illness, just as there had been a link between Addison's disease and the adrenal hormones? Dr. Cannon thought my father's ideas had sufficient enough merit to approve the research.

True to his training with Albright and Cannon, my father was looking for a physiological basis to his illness. He was seeking a biochemical explanation for his intense and terrifying moods.

I pictured him in his white coat, absorbed in his work at his laboratory. By then he knew the physiology of the adrenal glands very well. The glands sit at the top of the kidneys. Together, they weigh only a fraction of an ounce, but they can have a tremendous effect on a person's well-being. They are responsible for releasing hormones into the bloodstream in response to fear, stress, anger, or other excitement—the same hormones that cause the heart to race and the blood pressure to rise when we feel under threat. During his manic episodes, my father had experienced near ecstatic surges of excitement. He felt certain this could be connected to those glands, specifically the adrenal cortex—that part of the gland that mediates the rush of adrenaline, keeping it within normal range. My father reasoned that it was possible the adrenal cortex was malfunctioning in patients who were manic, causing uncontrolled and abnormal rushes of energy.

The first step, my father knew, was to ascertain whether the blood of acutely manic patients differed from that of healthy patients. For his experiments, he obtained blood from mental patients staying at the nearby McLean Hospital, keeping the vials of blood refrigerated at the laboratory, hopeful that if he could just unlock the secrets of their contents he might find some way of helping not only himself, but the many thousands of patients across the country suffering with manic depression.

Dr. Cannon had pioneered the study of the adrenal gland using laboratory cats. My father followed his lead. He had twenty cats in all, allowing him to divide them into two groups, ten for his test group and ten for the control group. First he sedated the two groups, removing their adrenal glands with a surgeon's quick precision. After the gland was removed, the cats' lives would be reduced to a span of no more than a few days. The cats in the control group were then injected with regular blood, while the cats in the test group were injected with blood from manic patients. My father's plan was "to determine whether or not these injections might lengthen the life of the animals." Early results proved promising: the cats injected with manic blood survived 40 percent longer than those injected with blood from nonmanic patients.

This breakthrough in his research arrived late in 1934. At this juncture, however, he was forced to put his investigations on hold. In November of that year, he experienced a second manic episode. He was admitted to McLean psychiatric hospital, the same hospital where he had obtained blood for his experiments.

McLean Hospital, 1934

On November 3, 1934, the patient suddenly became
over-active, euphoric, and excited. His hyper-
activity became extreme restlessness and sleep-
lessness. He had developed an idea for making
a million dollars through a suit against the
Westinghouse Electric Company who had apparently given him a defective machine. He worked
terribly hard. He was advised by his doctors to

go to McLean Hospital. He arrived at McLean on
November 11, 1934.

He remained in a wildly maniacal state for
ten days. When no physician was around he seemed
to lose all control. He became aggressive, com-
bative and very destructive. He smashed light
fixtures, windowpanes, furniture, some of which
he attempted to use as weapons. He broke a
transom with his hand, after which he had to
be restrained. After a brief period of quiet,
apologetic, cooperative behavior, the patient,
about twenty days after admission, had become
mildly depressed. In early December, he again was
quite active, mildly exuberant and enthusiastic.
The patient felt that he and his wife were not
very happy together. Two nights before admission
he had a long talk with his wife, at the end of
which she had stated that she hated him. He was
discharged from McLean after twenty-nine days at
the hospital, on December 10, 1934, as improved.

After his release, Dr. Cannon was gravely concerned. He felt
my father should hold off on laboratory work for the foreseeable
future. "Everybody has a critical stress which he can stand and
that varies greatly with individuals," Dr. Cannon wrote in a letter immediately after my father's release. "The prudent person is
one who learns by careful observation where that stress lies and
manages his life so that he lives within the limits. Of course,
research is exacting because animals have to be attended to, and
it is very likely to be exciting if results prove favorable. Both
these conditions are to be avoided, I believe, at present."

My father took Dr. Cannon's advice to heart. Beginning in

1935, his medical records confirm, he set aside his research and threw his energies into his private practice in Boston. Three years later, I was born. Although the letters make clear that my father was proud of his new family, conscientious in his work as a dermatologist, and stimulated by the interactions with his patients, he clearly missed his laboratory work. "It is sort of starvation to stay out of academic circles and deny one's self the privilege of doing scientific research," he wrote to Cannon. In the waning months of 1939, he wrote again to his mentor expressing his strong desire to resume his research on manic depression.

Dr. Cannon replied with increased caution. "I do not like to discourage anyone's enthusiasm," he wrote, "but in this present situation I should say that it would be wise to weigh carefully all the considerations before taking a step which may involve you in the expenditure of a large amount of money."

On December 19, 1940, my father again wrote to Dr. Cannon: "I have decided in my own heart that I am going to find a way of continuing these experiments—even if I have to build a laboratory in my home and use my own blood with Gretta's as a control. My mood to continue these experiments is recent and comes as a relief from these six years of meditating upon those unfinished experiments and of regretting the absence of time and courage to continue them."

Dr. Cannon was persuaded—in the next letter, he agreed to support the work. My father continued his laboratory research, intent on establishing a connection between his illness and the body's biochemistry. Again, blood he obtained from McLean was injected into cats with their adrenal glands removed. This time, my father observed that the manic cats lived five times longer than the control group.

In the early spring of 1942, my father completed a first draft of his article "Biochemical Component of the Manic-Depressive Psychosis."

"These experiments have provided biological evidence that the blood of manic patients may differ from the blood of healthy subjects," he wrote. He made clear that his findings were preliminary in nature, and that he had proven only that animals injected with manic blood behaved differently than animals injected with regular blood. His hope, however, was that his approach might create a significant shift in the study of manic depression.

"Perhaps this report will stimulate added interest in the manic psychosis as a physiological and general medical problem rather than as a purely psychological one. It may be hoped that other investigators will continue these studies."

Dr. Cannon responded with a very detailed letter with a long list of amendments. A reply to Cannon's suggestions came not from my father, but from my mother this time. It was May of 1942, and my father was unable to write. He was being held at the Boston Psychopathic Hospital, in the throes of another manic break. He stayed there for nine days.

On his release, my father continued to rework his article. He wrote to Dr. Means expressing the hope that his manuscript might soon be published. He described his recent confinement as "those ten days of dark psychiatry," and added, "I shall be willing to make whatever sacrifices are necessary to speed the progress of these experiments." The following year, he fell ill again, being readmitted to Boston Psychopathic Hospital before being transferred to Westborough for a stay of a month.

Toward the end of 1943, my father learned that his article

"Biochemical Component of the Manic-Depressive Psychosis" had finally been accepted for publication in the *Journal of Nervous and Mental Disease.* It was published in the spring of 1944, while he was being held again at Westborough.

My father had run out of time—the race to cure himself was lost. While he was locked away in hospital writing his manuscript, the Massachusetts medical board removed his license to practice medicine. From the confines of his cell, he could do nothing to promote his article. Many of his peers were away overseas in the war, so there was no one left to champion his discoveries. My father's research was quickly overlooked and, soon enough, forgotten.

CHAPTER TWENTY

My father had been convinced that there was a biochemical cause for his illness. Psychiatrists and other doctors caring for the mentally ill in 1944 were a long way from reaching a similar conclusion.

While my father was at Westborough—subjected to straight-jackets, cold packs, and solitary confinement—a Portuguese neurobiologist, Egas Moniz, was becoming famous for a new and radical brain surgery that he claimed could effectively treat mental illness. The surgery was called the lobotomy. Moniz and his followers believed that if the frontal lobes of the brain could be severed, then the patient's emotions could effectively be cut away. In the United States, the lobotomy's greatest proponent was the neurologist Dr. Walter Freeman, who helped popularize the procedure by traveling to state mental hospitals across the country, demonstrating the technique on patients while doctors and staff looked on.

My father would eventually receive his lobotomy in 1949, soon after Freeman visited the hospital where he was being held. Dr. Freeman's particular technique involved inserting an instrument shaped like an ice pick through the inner corners of the eye sockets, before moving the pick back and forth within the brain, as if scrambling eggs. After the surgery, it was observed that patients were less agitated, and therefore Freeman and his converts considered the operation successful. The vast majority of patients who received lobotomies, however, were permanently brain damaged and unable to function normally. Stripped of character, mobility, and energy, they were unrecognizable when compared to their former selves.

In 1949, the same year my father was lobotomized, Dr. Moniz won the Nobel Prize in Medicine. Over the next three years, somewhere in the region of fifty thousand Americans were subjected to the lobotomy "cure." With hindsight, it can be difficult to comprehend how so many respected medical professionals subscribed to such a brutal "solution." But doctors and families were desperate for hope. Nothing else was working. At that time, psychiatric patients occupied 55 percent of all hospital beds in America, and over half of those patients had been residents for over five years.

My father was no exception. In the years after he escaped from Westborough, his mental health only continued to worsen, and he bounced from hospital to hospital. After eight months at his parents' home in Dallas, he returned to Boston in early March 1945. A few days after his arrival—medical records confirm—my father paid us a late-night visit at our home. I must have slept through events as he broke our garage window, climbed inside, and drove away in the car he had once owned. Later in the night—my mother having reported the car as stolen—he was apprehended in Boston and turned over to the Newton police, who delivered him to Westborough once more. Soon after, he was transferred to the Bridgewater State Hospital for the Criminally Insane.

From there, my father wrote the following letter to his old friend and faculty advisor at Harvard, Dr. James Howard Means. It was Saturday, May 19, 1945.

Dear Dr. Means,

Life here on State Farm is not exactly an entrancing experience for more reasons than one, but it has taught me a lot about people "and things." I was arrested in front of Copley Plaza on charges of stealing my own car (now in Gretta's name). I was of course taken first to Boston police station and then thrown in a cell at Newton police station where I went berserk and became as wild as a jungle beast, tearing the plumbing out and raising Hell in general.

After transference to Westborough I grew vastly worse and "tore the place to pieces," was put in a straight jacket and beaten unmercifully. Arrived at State Farm Prison Hospital three days later with Ecchymoses from head to foot—my nose bruised and swollen, my left eye black down to middle left cheek.

Here I am among a lot of patients and assorted criminals and as usual my psychiatrists and lawyers claim they can do nothing for me. My lawyer, Talcott M. Banks Jr of Palmer, Dodge & Co. wants me to leave Massachusetts permanently—and I have become reconciled to this fate. I came back merely to see my children and friends. Oh boy what a pack o' trouble! So I guess it's goodbye forever to dear ol' New England. I'll try out Texas or Michigan again. There are plenty of pretty girls in Texas and elsewhere. I'll marry again and have more chicks and maybe I'll pine less for my daughters, who bind me to New England, where I want them to stay.

Please write or come to see me.

Ever sincerely,

PERRY

Dr. Means replied on June 1, 1945:

Dear Perry,

Many thanks for yours of May 19th. I had heard the unhappy news that you had been transferred to Bridgewater. It's most unfortunate, but I fear inevitable, if you cannot manage to get under cover voluntarily in the brief space of time that free choice remains to you during the prodromal stages of an attack, that you will be treated more or less as you have been this time and others. I suppose society just isn't organized to deal with the kind of problem your case presents when you enter upon a manic phase of your disease.

About going to Texas, I don't believe I can advise you wisely. It seems possible that a totally new environment there might diminish the chance of relapses, but one cannot be sure.

As I see it, you are suffering from a chronic malady, characterized by remissions and relapses, cause and specific treatment for which are as yet quite unknown. Dr. Tillotson thinks electric shock treatments offer something. I just don't know. Aside from that, I think regardless of where you are, the important thing is to have constant psychiatric control. If you could bring yourself to let your psychiatrist tell you when to get under cover, and obey him, you might spare yourself and your friends, a lot of grief. One thing you could

do when you are discharged is to go on the water wagon for
life. But you haven't been willing to do this, and no one can
force you.

> *With kindest regards,*
> *HOWARD MEANS*

It was the last time my father ever heard from his loyal
friend and advisor. Like so many of my father's friends and colleagues, Dr. Means was no longer able to maintain a connection
with someone so unstable. My father's mental illness had finally
severed their many years of close friendship.

From this point on, my father entered a period of marked
isolation. For the next three years, he remained institutionalized
in various hospitals in Massachusetts. Eventually he was transferred to Butler Hospital, a much smaller and well-respected
sanatorium in Providence, Rhode Island. By now, the records
make obvious that he was severely ill.

Butler Hospital, 1948–1949

The patient spends a considerable amount of
time talking to the other patients about murder
and explained to them how legal murder could be
accomplished.

At one time he told his physician of an experiment he had performed in which, through the
action of delta rays, two ten-pound cats were
combined into one cat weighing ten pounds. When
asked to explain this, he said, "I don't know
about this. I'm just telling you the facts. This
is what we did." When asked to explain this further, he said that this was most secretive.

The patient's paranoid ideation concerns abstract matters, systematized into what he calls "neo-physics." In this system various types of rays can be made to fuse the bodies of 500 men into one body, or fuse a male and female animal into one hermaphrodite animal. Also, as relates to himself, he at times states that he was in a "super-intelligence" service of the government during the late war fused into the personality of other men, and in this capacity saw action on all the great battlefields and was in all of the enemy capitols. Through these experiences he, or one of the many personalities that had been placed within him, was wounded and killed numberless times.

Several times while in seclusion he claimed he was a horse and at other times would roar like a lion. Only once was he assaultive, when in a moment of panic he suddenly hit two attendants. He immediately apologized profusely and asked to be secluded. Other than this his destructiveness was in terms of his own clothing that he would rip off.

He once explained a hemorrhoid that he had developed as caused by Communist super-intelligence service beaming rays from many miles off at his rectum, and the converging beams squeezed out the hemorrhoid. He considered that since no one in the hospital was responsible for his difficulty, they could not have been expected to prevent him from being harmed.

My father stayed at Butler for one year, after which time he was released to his family in Dallas for a brief period of freedom. In September 1949, he decided to pack his bags and begin walking across the state into Mexico, where he was determined to start his life over. A week later, he woke up in the hospital, severely beaten, but with no recollections of events. After he had recovered, he hitchhiked south, until he reached Galveston's city limits. The police found him, disheveled and bloody, walking along the highway, whereupon he was soon transferred to Galveston State Hospital.

Galveston State Hospital, 1949

Dr. Baird's stay in the hospital was a long, rough and rugged one. It was punctuated by frequent moves from the disturbed ward to the open floor and back to the disturbed ward. Almost immediately after coming into the hospital, Dr. Baird's behavior became quite frankly psychotic and he was placed on electro-shock therapy three times a week and deep insulin comas every day.

For a while, Dr. Baird seemed to be doing very fine with his treatments. However, suddenly he relapsed again, began talking about people walking in the hall in just a certain manner that was intended to annoy him. He also spoke of how they communicated signals to one another by the way that they shuffled their feet.

From here on he went back again to his frankly psychotic behavior. Altogether Dr. Baird received about 60 full-hour insulin comas and received a total of 33 electro-shock treatments. After this very extensive course of treatment, Dr. Baird's clinical presentation was certainly no better than it had been when he first came to this

```
    hospital, and it was felt that further treatment
    with electro and insulin shock would be useless.
        It was finally decided that lobotomy was the
    only procedure that could possibly help this
    patient's psychosis.
```

So began the concerted campaign by the doctors at Galveston to persuade my father's family to agree to a lobotomy. During the fall and winter of 1949, a series of letters (preserved with his medical records) went back and forth between my father's family and his doctors at Galveston. The doctors' advice was that my father should undergo a lobotomy as soon as possible. My grandparents were initially opposed, but my uncles were easier to convince. My father had been subjected to every other treatment available, from cold packs and straightjackets to insulin-induced comas and electric shock therapy. On December 15, 1949, my father's brother, Philip, wrote to the doctors at Galveston: "My feeling is that we have done everything we can do and if your operation is successful it will be a momentous occasion for all of us."

My uncles signed the consent form, with my grandparents' approval.

They must have felt they had no other choice. My father's medical records during the weeks leading up to his surgery make clear that his mental state was as compromised as ever.

Galveston State Hospital, 1949

```
September 18—Can tell very interesting but
slightly fantastic tales. Seems eager to display
```

medical knowledge but in most of discussion will suddenly switch conversation to Aztec history.

October 23—Apparently having delusions. "There was a great catastrophe last night. There is water everywhere and Galveston is apparently floating away. It has broken away from its foundation, you know it is only an island, and we are floating away out to the sea." Patient is very upset about this. He is very disarrayed in his dress and is very concerned about us floating away.

December 7—Very confused this morning. Has talked about being on a boat, various different sports, asking us to make arrangements for a racehorse so he could enter a jumping contest in New England.

December 19—Playing dominoes with other patients. Quiet today. Apologetic to excess at every mistake he makes. Wrote prescription for rash on another patient. Patient was playing dominoes with another patient when he started crying quietly.

December 20—Patient is confused and appears agitated. Doubles up his fist as if he'd like to hit someone. He threatened attendants in kitchen this a.m. Chases attendant with a fork.

December 22—Helped nurse make beds.

. . .

On December 23, 1949, my father underwent a prefrontal bilateral lobotomy. His records contain copies of both the permits for treatment and the operation notes, and go on to describe a good but gradual recovery, until he was discharged to his brother Philip on February 23, 1950.

After my father's release from Galveston, I have no other records, no manuscript notes, and no more letters to or from friends. He seems to have stopped writing altogether. When I interviewed my father's friend Frank Shaw, he told me he had seen Perry only once after his lobotomy, when my father returned to Boston for his sole visit to me. "We were all shocked," Shaw told me. "He really wasn't Perry anymore. All the fire had gone out of him."

My father spent the next few years recuperating in Texas. Early in 1959, a colleague of his from medical school found him a job as an ambulance attendant in Detroit and my uncle helped finance a move there. My father was living in a small room in a low-rent boardinghouse when, six weeks after his arrival in Detroit, one of the other tenants found him, drowned in his bathtub, after a seizure most likely brought on by his brain surgery.

I applied for his death certificate. The date of his death was May 4, 1959. The cause of death was listed as "asphyxia by drowning." On the same certificate his occupation is listed as "Doctor." He was fifty-five years old.

CHAPTER TWENTY-ONE

I resolved to write a book about my father's life and work that would include his manuscript and the information I had uncovered about his research on manic depression. There were many times when I retreated from the task, overwhelmed. At other times, I simply came to a halt, assuming I had progressed as far as was possible. But the writing process was also marked by many moments of great fortune and coincidence, each event giving the arduous work an irresistible momentum.

A lucky break came in the summer of 1996. Early in the year, I'd arranged to have a synopsis of my father's manuscript published in *Psychiatric Services,* a journal of the American Psychiatric Association. To my delight, I was able to include the first citation of my father's article on manic depression ever to appear in print. That same July, I received a letter from Dr. Elliot S. Valenstein, professor emeritus of psychology and neuroscience at the University of Michigan and a reader of *Psychiatric Services.*

"After finishing reading your synopsis," he told me, "I walked over to our medical library and read a copy of your father's paper on a possible 'biochemical component of manic-depressive psychosis.' Your father's paper was published five years ahead of John Cade's paper about lithium treatment of mania. You may know that John Cade who was a virtually unknown Australian physician at the time, had injected urine from manic patients into guinea pigs, believing as your father did that he would find a biochemical explanation of mania."

Enclosed with the letter was Dr. Valenstein's book *Great*

and Desperate Cures: The Rise and Decline of Psychosurgery and Other Radical Treatments. Spurred on by our correspondence, I soon located a short biography of John Cade in a book on mental illness and its treatment. While my father was being held at Westborough, Cade began his famous series of experiments, working out of a disused hospital kitchen that he converted into a makeshift laboratory. As Dr. Valenstein had noted, Cade's breakthrough came when he began to inject urine samples from manic patients into guinea pigs. After taking the urine and adding lithium urate—a naturally occurring mineral similar to salt—in the hope of reducing toxicity, Cade noticed a remarkable side effect. Not only did the lithium reduce toxicity, it also seemed to have a calming effect on his laboratory animals. Perhaps the same would be true if lithium were given to human subjects. Cade ingested small amounts of lithium to observe any adverse side effects before beginning trials on ten patients at the hospital who were manic depressive. The results were extraordinary. The lithium had the same calming effect on his patients that he had seen in his laboratory animals. Cade now ventured that mania was caused by a deficiency in lithium. His results were detailed in his paper "Lithium Salts in the Treatment of Psychotic Excitement," published in the *Medical Journal of Australia* in 1949. After a series of more extensive trials, lithium was later heralded as the first truly effective medication for mental illness.

Cade's mood-stabilizing drug finally arrived in the United States in 1970—too late for my father—and remains one of the standard treatments for manic depression or bipolar disorder, as it is now more commonly known. Cade went on to a long and much-lauded career, becoming a distinguished fellow of the American Psychiatric Association. In 1985 the National Institute of Mental Health estimated that Cade's discovery had saved the world somewhere in the region of $17.5 billion in medical costs.

I couldn't help but hold up my father's research alongside Dr. Cade's. Like Cade, my father believed that some biochemical abnormality or deficiency might be in part responsible for manic depression. While Cade's experiments led to one of the key scientific discoveries of our times, my father's research was forever halted by his illness. It is impossible to know how my father's work would have developed if he had been given more time, but I can't help but feel that he had come tantalizingly close.

I was, of course, excited by these revelations, but they also left me with a profound sense of loss. If my father had been born a few years later, he could have benefited from Dr. Cade's discovery of lithium as an effective treatment for mania. And perhaps, for that golden time, I could have grown up with a father.

. . .

I continued to make discoveries, small and large.

Not all the revelations were welcome ones. It was difficult to conceive that the manic, raving patient I found in the medical records coexisted with a wife and two young children in the narrow confines of our home, with its thin wooden walls. Long-buried memories began to resurface. I could remember lying upstairs in my bed and hearing my father's Victrola down below, a party in full swing, the music so loud that the walls of my bedroom vibrated. Then, the music faded and voices were raised in argument. I can recall the sound of my mother's cries. My parents' divorce papers cite "cruel and unusual treatment," and my father's medical records make clear that he was violent while held in hospitals. For years, I have carried with me a memory of ketchup splattered on the walls of our kitchen at Clovelly Road. Now I believe that my father likely attacked my mother during one of those arguments. I still find it very hard to reconcile the father that I loved with the terribly sick man who must have created such misery and havoc in our home.

. . .

By now, my mother was in her mid-eighties. As my work on the book progressed, I grew increasingly concerned about her health. She was forgetting basic information. She often repeated herself and was frequently confused. She found she needed to write a list to remind her of what was going to happen on any given day. Once, when visiting at her home, I went into the kitchen to make a telephone call. When I came back, she greeted me as though I had just arrived. Soon after that, she was diagnosed with early-stage senile dementia and agreed to move to an assisted-living facility just outside Boston.

Before moving, she went through her house and reduced the number of her possessions. But she kept her many photograph albums, feeling that they would provide her a connection to the past. She stored these on the bottom shelf of her small bookcase in her new home, and each time I visited, we would sit on her living room couch and spread the albums out on the coffee table. The images went back to her childhood years. The momentary joy she experienced while remembering her youth was worth each visit. In the later albums there were only a few images of my father. One photograph was of him dressed in a well-tailored business suit. Another showed him in his handsome riding clothes, ready for a foxhunt. There was even a snapshot of my father and me together, riding his horse Viking. When we reached this particular album, my mother turned the pages as quickly as she could.

Her health continued to deteriorate. Whereas in the past she could write lists of what to do each day, clutching them in her hand or placing them in the pocket of her skirt, she was no longer able to corral her thoughts. As often as possible, I would travel down from Vermont to visit with her. Despite her scattered attention, my mother was always neatly dressed. I can see her now in her usual round-collared blouse, wraparound skirt, and button-down sweater. Her stockings were a bit wrinkled, but she continued her weekly visit to the hairdresser.

During this period of her decline, I found my mother was finally less resistant to talking about the past. One day, when I told her I had been investigating my father's research, she turned to me.

"He was so hoping to find the cause of his insanity," she stated slowly. "He just didn't succeed."

I pressed her further, but she only smiled and changed the subject.

On my next visit, I asked her if my father had ever gotten into trouble with the police.

"Oh yes," she replied. "It wasn't unusual for me to have to leave the house in the early-morning hours to bail him out of jail."

She went on to remember the time she had to buy new uniforms for the policemen who had fished my father out of the duck pond in the Boston Public Gardens.

On another visit, I broached the subject of the noises I had heard from my bedroom upstairs in Clovelly Road.

"Mother, you know that I often heard you and father fighting downstairs while you thought I was sleeping."

"Oh no, dear," she insisted. "You couldn't have done. The walls were well insulated."

· · ·

One day I asked her to tell me how they met, which prompted one of our longer discussions.

"I was a student at Boston's Leland Powers School of Dramatic Art," she remembered. "I was twenty years old. A friend called and asked me to go on a blind date. I said: 'I never go on blind dates.' My friend said, 'I've got two doctors on my hands. We're going dancing.' I didn't have anything to do, so I said, 'Okay.'"

One doctor was Marshall Bartlett, our old family friend whom I had visited to learn more about my father. The other was Perry Baird.

"It was Prohibition," my mother went on. "The doctors brought some alcohol from the hospital. We went to a hotel off Copley Square for dancing. I danced most of the night with Perry. I had a wonderful time. Perry called me right after I got home that night. I started seeing him, and Marsh stepped out of the picture."

"What was he like?"

"Perry Baird was *fascinating,* just plain fun. He spoke softly, with a slight Texan accent. After I met your father, he was all I was interested in."

I asked if she remembered when my father asked her to marry him.

"Yes, of course," she replied. "It was on Newbury Street. He put a diamond ring on my finger. It was his grandmother's. Afterward he slipped into a phone booth and called his grandmother. He said: 'I just put your ring on my dear Gretta's finger.' I can hear those words just as plain now as then."

I sensed from her smiles that my parents had once, long ago, been very much in love and had been happy, for a time.

. . .

As I grew ever more immersed in my research, I realized that in order to have the fullest picture of what had happened between my parents, I needed to have a better understanding of my grandfather's mental illness. When my mother met Perry on a blind date in Boston, did she recognize something of her long-lost father in him?

I applied for Henry's—my grandfather's—medical records from the mental institution in Norristown, Pennsylvania, where he spent most of his life, in the hopes that the records would offer additional insights. As I scanned the pages, the following entry stopped me in my tracks:

Norristown State Hospital, 1943

```
June 8: Patient, in a hypo-manic state, is vis-
ited today by his son-in-law, Dr. Perry Baird,
who put him on a bus to visit his daughter in Mas-
sachusetts. Patient was returned on a train from
Boston on June 24, 1943. He was most apologetic.
```

So my father had helped his father-in-law escape and gain a few weeks of respite from his hospital cell. A year later, my own father was locked away at Westborough. At this point, my mother shut down, refusing to speak of what had happened, exactly as her own mother had done.

. . .

Beginning in 1997, my mother experienced several mini-strokes, which further compromised the quality of her life and made her increasingly forgetful. Physically she looked just the same, but she became less careful about her appearance, and much slower in her motions. In 1999, I was called by the facility where she lived, Clark House, and told she had slipped into a semiconscious state. I traveled to see her, wondering if it would be the last of such journeys. Upon arrival, I went directly to her room and found her resting, unresponsive. The nurse told me that her heart was still strong and reassured me that I could return to Vermont later that afternoon.

Early the following day, the nurse called again to say her condition had weakened and that I should return. My sister was on vacation, so I called my daughter and two nieces and asked them to meet me at Clark House. Although my mother was barely conscious, the four of us quietly spoke to her. We assured her that all was well in the family and that we understood it was time for her to go. Occasionally her eyes opened and she turned slightly on her bed. At times she appeared unsettled, restless.

After a while, my daughter and her cousins went out of the room to find some nourishment. I sat at my mother's side, continuing to quietly speak to her. Suddenly, she opened her eyes wide, looking directly into my own.

"I apologize," she said, her voice suddenly strong and direct. "I am very sorry." Her eyes closed slowly. After that, her restlessness seemed to ease. Within an hour she was gone. It was January 17, 1999.

In the weeks to come, I attempted to understand why she had apologized to me in those final hours. Could she have been acknowledging that she could have shared more of my father's story with me, and that now it was too late?

My mother's death presented me with a stark choice. I could carry our family secrets to the grave, as she had done—like her mother before her—or I could attempt to hold them up to the light and air.

. . .

For the next decade, I kept returning to this book. I had retired from my job at the hospital and was becoming ever more engrossed by new work with a local charitable foundation, and so the writing progressed in fits and starts. Then, in the winter of 2011, I received a call from my daughter, Meg. She had been assisting one of her sons with a homework assignment that required him to trace his family's genealogy. Meg had described the various branches of our family and their history to my grandson, and then Googled my father's name for good measure. This was how she discovered that a book existed containing a reference to my father and his research. It was by Dr. Elliot Valenstein, and it was titled *Blaming the Brain: The Truth about Drugs and Mental Health.* Meg read Dr. Valenstein's words aloud to me on the telephone: "John Cade was not the first person to search for a biochemical basis of mania by injecting experimental animals with fluids obtained from mental patients. Perry Baird, at the time a successful Boston dermatologist who suffered from a manic depressive disorder, injected blood from a manic patient into adrenalectomized animals."

Blaming the Brain had recently been reprinted with its references amended to include my father's name and his achievement. Dr. Valenstein also cited my father's 1944 article and my synopsis of his manuscript in *Psychiatric Services* in 1996.

My daughter was jubilant. So was I. Perry Baird's name had found its way into medical history, in a footnote, it's true, but nonetheless his contribution had been recognized.

. . .

During this same period, I came across a letter I had never noticed before, tucked among the pages of my father's manuscript. It was written in August of 1944, soon after his escape from Westborough, and it was addressed to Reverend Corny Trowbridge, our minister at Chestnut Hill. I remembered Corny's kindness to my father, visiting him while he was in the hospital and sending him a copy of a book about St. Francis. Evidently my father had begun a correspondence with the reverend soon after.

In the letter, my father returns to the idea that his life may hold some greater purpose:

Dear Corny,

Your letter written from the Saranac Inn was a powerful communication. As with all of your letters, I have found it profitable to read your last letter several times and I have found much enjoyment in listening to what you had to say. I find great comfort in your belief that my recent reversal of fortune may lead "in the end to something of great worth." The stormy course of my life during the last twelve years has proved to me that many good fortunes lie concealed in apparent disasters. Certainly in wrestling with adversity one learns to attain added courage and strength, and one learns to find beauty wherever it may be found regardless of the background.

Strange as it may seem, my periods of so-called illness are usually associated with certain productive powers not ordinarily available to me. Certain new abilities have come to light during my manic attacks. Perhaps this is a clue to the "something of great worth" which may come out of these misfortunes. Out of the cauldron of despair, came forth a rather lengthy manuscript which one expert describes as a "magnificent work of art." I am not convinced that the book deserves this amount of praise but I do know that in it, I have attained a style of expression that was available to me only during "illness."

To finish this book is the one thing that I most want to do in life and I am working on the project now. It will involve telling the story of manic-depressive insanity, weaving in the lives of many really notable people who have suffered from it, recounting my own story. There will be commentaries upon modern hospital care with its queer barbarities and shortcomings, messages for friends and relatives of persons so afflicted, lines of reasoning, argument and education, built up in the hope of improving the general viewpoint about this type of insanity, perhaps improving general tolerance for it.

To reduce or remove certain prejudices would make worthwhile all efforts spent in writing the book. The book is already quite a long one and yet I haven't come anywhere near the end. There will come a time to cut out parts here and there. It will probably require several more years to complete the job in the right way.

Here the letter ends. My father never signed his letter to Corny, nor did he send it. As with so much of his life's work, the letter remained unfinished. Yet I find great redemption in its survival and marvel that it has somehow found its way to me, and now to you, through the pages of our book.

I n March of 2013, nearly twenty years after I first inherited
my father's papers, I traveled to New York to meet my editor at Crown Publishers, an imprint of Random House. The
city sky was still wintry and gray, freshened by an icy wind
coming in from the river. I approached the glass entrance to
1745 Broadway, the headquarters of Penguin Random House,
with feelings of nervous excitement, emerging through revolv-
ing doors into a large, sleek lobby with soaring ceilings.

On either side of me stood vast, gleaming glass bookshelves,
each illuminated from within, with shelves holding row upon
row of books. I walked over to one of the cases, scanning the

spines, reading the names of countless titles and authors. Here were old Modern Library editions of Hawthorne and Melville, an original copy of *Ulysses* by James Joyce, and of Dr. Seuss's *Oh, the Places You'll Go.* I even glimpsed a name I recognized very well: William Styron, whose *Darkness Visible* was one of the early books that had given me an understanding of mental illness.

I paused a moment longer, still trying to absorb the enormity of the moment. I thought of my father's own journey to New York in 1932, in the middle of his first severe manic episode, when he had been determined to meet with an editor and find a publisher for his writing. I thought of Westborough, where he wrote his book, the book he had hoped would offer a window into his devastating condition. I remembered all the years his manuscript had lain in an old briefcase in my cousin's garage, forgotten by all but a few.

My father's desire for publication was finally being fulfilled. I am not someone who is prone to emotional displays—my mother dubbed me the ice princess with good reason—but standing in the lobby that morning, I felt tears, both unexpected and happy, springing to my eyes.

After the meeting in New York, I returned to Vermont to finish preparing the manuscript. My editor had asked me to go back into my archive of my father's writings and to transcribe every single word that I could find there. I made many new discoveries during this time, scraps of writings I had originally overlooked, medical records I'd never completely scrutinized, letters I'd only scanned but never mined fully for information. In the coming weeks, I sat on my living room floor surrounded by a circle of paper stacks.

At moments, it was as if I was reading my father's words for the first time. More than ever, I felt aware of the terrifying power of his manic energy. I began to fully acknowledge both the violence done to him while he was held in hospitals and that he had exerted on his surroundings and others. I faced emotions that I had held in abeyance for most of my life, dwelling on everything my father had lost to his illness. So much had been taken from him: his family, his business, his home, his reputation, his vocation, and his mind. I allowed myself to finally imagine the enormity of those subtractions.

I thought about how my father had prevailed with his experiments in his research laboratory, no matter how many times his work was interrupted by his incarcerations in mental institutions. I considered his determination to write his book despite so much heartbreak and despair. I read and reread his words, assembling the pages as if piecing together a broken mirror in which I was beginning to find my own image reflected.

I found myself taking more walks than usual, staring into space, staying awake at night, feeling dazed when the morning came. I realized I was experiencing a momentous shift in the foundation of my identity. I had spent my lifetime searching, wondering, deciphering. Now the defining mystery of my father had been put to rest. I knew who he was, what he had endured, and what had been his legacy. One day, sitting at my desk, pausing from my work for a moment to stare into the dark green leaves of the ficus tree that I had brought into the house from the winter cold, I was struck by the extraordinary timing of it all. I had just turned seventy-five years old. I had come to these discoveries late in life, but it had not been too late after all.

Notes

page 15: **going to The Country Club** My father capitalizes the definite article when he refers to The Country Club, where he was a member. The venerable club just outside Boston was the first of its kind in the nation, and the club and its members capitalize the definite article in its name to this day.

page 203: **Harvard Medical School graduate** Days after my father's death in 1959, my stepfather happened to meet Dr. Thomas Lanman, director of alumni relations at Harvard Medical School's Alumni Association. My stepfather mentioned that his wife's former husband—a Harvard Medical School alum—had just passed away. A few days later, Dr. Lanman wrote my stepfather the following letter:

> I have looked into the matter of degrees at the Medical School . . . Perry received his M.D. in 1928, *magna cum laude,* and I believe that this was given not only because of his high academic standing, but for his brilliant work "in a special field," for he wrote an excellent thesis in the field of physiology. I think we are entirely correct in saying that he received the highest academic honors ever awarded at that time to any medical school graduate.
>
> However, I have no doubt that he would have been awarded a degree *summa cum laude* but for the fact that the University did not give a *summa cum laude* in medicine. It was about 1940 or 1942 that the Corporation and the Board of Overseers granted the authority to the Faculty of the Harvard Medical School to award an M.D. degree *summa cum laude.* There have been only two *summa*s since then. Just why the Corporation felt no doctor should be awarded a degree *summa cum laude* until 1940 I am entirely unable to state. In any case, Perry received the highest degree possible at that time.

page 203: **applied for my father's medical records** I obtained my father's medical records a year before the Health Insurance Portability and Accountability Act (HIPAA) was introduced. Had I waited until 1996, when the new rules around patient privacy were rolled out, I might never have been able to obtain these documents.

page 217: **the operation successful** Information on Walter Freeman and lobotomies is taken from *Great and Desperate Cures: The Rise and Decline of Psychosurgery and Other Radical Cures for Mental Illness* by Elliot S. Valenstein (1986).

page 218: **lobotomy "cure"** From *Last Resort: Psychosurgery and the Limits of Medicine* by Jack D. Pressman (1998).

page 229: **$17.5 billion in medical costs** Information on John Cade comes from *The Australian Dictionary of Biography,* Vol. 13 (1993).

Acknowledgments

As many authors know, writing is a lonely occupation. After years of working alone, my circumstances changed with a single phone call. In the spring of 2012, Amity Shlaes, the author and syndicated columnist, asked me what I was doing after retiring from my trusteeship of a small non-profit. Meekly, I replied that I was writing a book. The next thing I knew Amity had introduced me to her good friend, Carol Mann, of the eminent Carol Mann Agency, who agreed to become my agent.

Carol's calm guidance, perception, and encouragement became essential. Wisely, Carol assigned me an editor, the talented Eve Claxton. Enter the smart and determined Domenica Alioto of Crown Publishing. In December she spoke with Carol's able assistant Eliza Dreier, who alerted her to my father's manuscript. Soon after, Domenica and Crown agreed to publish our book. Thank you to Amity, Carol, Eliza, Eve, and Domenica for believing in *He Wanted the Moon*.

There were many individuals who helped bring the development of the book to fruition. Howard Coffin assisted in the early days of creation and discovery. Audrey Brown brought a fresh eye to the material. Among the early readers of the manuscript were: Susan Diamond, Mary Beardsley Fenn, Susan Haffenreffer, Cassie Horner, Truett Moore, Jane Rabb, Sheila Tanzer, Sally Thursby, and Robin B. Osborne, Ph.D. Dr. Osborne is also my therapist and it was she who suggested that I write a synopsis of my father's work for the book section of a psychiatric journal.

Jeffrey L. Geller, M.D., M.P.H., who served on the editorial board of the journal, allowed Robin's idea to become a reality. It was this journal that Dr. Elliot S. Valenstein read and realized the historic significance of one of my father's scientific papers. I am deeply grateful to each of you.

None of the above could have taken place if not for the discovery of my father's onionskin manuscript. In April 1994 I traveled to Texas and met with my uncle L. P. Baird, my father's youngest brother. It was he who told me of the existence of my father's work. Thank you, Uncle Philip. My deep gratitude also goes to my cousin, Randy Baird, and his wife, Karen McLinden, who for many years kept these papers safe. Thank you for entrusting them to my care. Without them there would be no *He Wanted the Moon*.

Without interviewing the following people, the personal side of my father's life would never have emerged: Barbara Bartlett, Dr. Marshall Bartlett, Dr. Bradford Cannon, Virginia Fenno, and Francis G. Shaw. A special nod to Mrs. Fenno, for it was she who said, as I turned to leave her home, "You know, Mimi, he wanted the moon."

The never-ending support of my family and friends sustained me through this long expedition: Gregory Baker, Patricia Higginson Biggar, Anne Bourne, Sally Ryder Brady, Margaret Davis, Margaret Edwards, Deborah Ellis, Bonnie Davis Gerrard, Kurt and Phyllis Gerrish, Teresa Golding, Patsy Highberg, Dan and Deb Jantzen, Sarwar Kashmeri, Deborah Kell, Tom and Diana Hayes, George Cabot Lee II, Richard Shattuck Lee, Deborah Morgan Luquer, Betty Masterson, Harold McLaughlin, Garda Meyer, Barnes Newberry, Giovanna Peebles, Frank Procopio, Sarah Reeves, Dr. Joseph M. Rosen, Catherine Baird

Smith, Nina Rosselli Del Turco, Gay Travers, Susie White-hurst, and Mary Stewart Wilson. Thanks also to Horst Dresler and Alex Kim at Anything Printed in Woodstock for the many copies and image scans they completed for me in the course of this project.

The incredible work of Kate Bradley will live down the years. Kate graciously took on the job of typing my father's entire manuscript. We had a tight schedule. Through the cold of those winter days of 2013, many nightmares, and lots of chocolate, she deciphered each and every word. We made the deadline. Thank you, Miss Kate.

Special recognition goes to Dr. Radford C. Tanzer, for not only knowing my father, but for telling me so; and Dr. William D. Morain, for obtaining the correspondence between my father and Dr. Walter B. Cannon. I had the pleasure of working for these two doctors and who could have imagined they would play such an important role in sorting out the threads of my father's life.

One of the stars in my universe is Domenica Alioto, my editor and guru at Crown Publishing. Her .unique vision and intuition saw to it that my father's work would see the light of day. Nothing was spared as she gathered many talented people around *He Wanted the Moon*. Her clear vision for this book remained an inspiration through the writing and editing process. Thank you, my friend.

Thank you to Barbara Sturman, our book designer, who took manuscript pages, photographs, text, and medical records, unifying them in pages of great elegance and sophistication. Much credit is due to Elena Giavaldi for designing a book cover that conveyed the many threads of the story inside. Thanks also to our devoted production editor Ada Yonenaka, our production manager Heather Williamson, and our exacting copyeditor Rosalie Wiedros (whose appreciation for this book showed in the extraordinary attention she gave to its every word).

The Crown publicity and marketing teams are unrivaled. Thanks to Annsley Rosner, Lauren Kuhn, Jay Sones, and Danielle Crabtree for the attention and intelligence they brought to the task of alerting the world to *He Wanted the Moon*. Thanks also to the superb Crown sales team. And of course, to our publisher, Molly Stern, for her superlative leadership—and for giving me the extraordinary opportunity of seeing my father's words in print.

And then there is the marvelous Eve Claxton, my expert in all things that make editing an art. Her first words to me were, "Your story knocked my socks off." Well, Eve, you have knocked my socks off. Your never-ending wisdom, patience, and understanding helped make the months of work fly. We faithfully spoke on Fridays at 4 p.m., a day and time that will always bring a smile to my face. Thank you, Eve, for everything tangible and intangible.

And lastly, from my children's point of view, the evolution of the book was a significant undertaking. During the days of discovery, they showed grace and compassion in trying to assimilate the facts I was carefully sending their way. It is my hope that by understanding their grandfather's victories and misfortunes, it will allow them to gain a better insight into our family history, and, at the same time give them a perspective that will enhance their lives. It is with the deepest love possible that I thank Jake and Meg for sticking by me all these years.

Photograph Credits

Page iv (Dr. Perry Baird's manuscript stack): Frank Procopio, Woodstock, Vermont

Page 27 (postcard of Westborough State Hospital): Perkins and Butler Inc. Worcester, Massachusetts

Page 99 (postcard of Baldpate Inn): W.R.M Haverhill, Massachusetts

All other photographs: Baird Family Collection

Source Credits

All manuscript pages, correspondence, and medical records of
Dr. Perry Baird are courtesy of Mimi Baird.

Grateful acknowledgment is made to the following for
permission to reprint previously published material:

Copyright Clearance Center: Excerpt from "Biochemical
Component of the Manic-Depressive Psychosis" by Perry C.
Baird, Jr., M.D. (*The Journal of Nervous and Mental Disease,*
April 1994). Reprinted by permission of Wolters Kluwer
Health, rights administered by Copyright Clearance Center.

The Dallas Morning News: "Obituary of Perry C. Baird"
(May 1959). Reprinted by permission of *The Dallas Morning
News.*

Harvard Alumni Association: Excerpt from a letter by
Dr. Thomas Lanman. Reprinted by permission of the Harvard
Alumni Association.

The Harvard Medical Library: Excerpts from the letters
of Perry C. Baird (Papers of Walter B. Cannon [H MS
c40, box 110] and James Howard Means [GA 54, box 1]).
Reprinted by permission of The Harvard Medical Library in
the Francis A. Countway Library of Medicine.

Dr. Elliot S. Valenstein: Excerpt from a letter by Dr. Elliot S.
Valenstein to Mimi Baird. Reprinted by permission of
Dr. Elliot S. Valenstein.

About the Authors

MIMI BAIRD, a Bostonian, is a graduate of Colby-Sawyer College. After working in the Dean's Office at the Harvard Graduate School of Education, she later moved to Woodstock, Vermont, where she worked as a manager at the Dartmouth-Hitchcock Medical Center. This is where she met a surgeon who had once known her father, a meeting that prompted her quest to finally understand her father's life and legacy. Her trusteeship at the President Calvin Coolidge Memorial Foundation led to the building of the President Calvin Coolidge Museum and Educational Center in Vermont. Mimi has two children and four grandchildren. This is her first book.

EVE CLAXTON was born in London and moved to New York in 1995. She has been instrumental in creating six works of nonfiction as a cowriter or ghostwriter, and is the editor of *The Book of Life,* an anthology of memoir. She has also worked for StoryCorps, the National Oral History Project, sourcing and recording stories for the broadcast segment on NPR and for the organization's books. Eve lives with her husband and three children in Brooklyn.

About the Type

The voice of Mimi Baird was set in Garamond 3; her father's, in Golden Days; and the medical records, in Prestige 12 Pitch.

The modern-day version of Garamond 3 was created by leading American type designer Morris Fuller Benton (1872–1948) in 1917 and 1936, based on the much earlier work of French printer Jean Jannon (1580–1635). Garamond 3 exemplifies the elegance and readability of French Renaissance style.

Based on retro sans-serif type from the 1950s, Golden Days was designed by Canadian typographer Lloyd Springer (b. 1966) and released by his company, TypeArt Foundry Inc., in 2002.

American typographer Clayton Smith designed Prestige 12 Pitch as a typewriter face for IBM in 1953. The font was introduced in digital form by Bitstream forty years later.

HE WANTED
THE MOON

A Conversation with
Mimi Baird

Q: Tell me about the process of writing *He Wanted the Moon*. How long did it take?

A: The writing of *He Wanted the Moon* took about twenty years, with many stops and starts along the way. At first, I wrote notes scribbled on odd scraps of paper: bank deposit slips, yellow lined legal paper, newspaper, magazines, and the back of business cards. I quickly realized that—in order to avoid losing these insights—I needed to enter them, chronologically, into my computer.

I kept up my research into my father's life, following every lead that came my way; watching in fascination as a story began to emerge. At a certain point, I began consolidating the scraps of information into chapters, constantly naming and renaming each one, before finally rewriting the episodes to create a more dramatic approach. I wrote about three versions, the last of which got me through my literary agent's door.

Q: What were the hardest parts of writing it?

A: One of the hardest aspects was maintaining the

necessary emotional distance in order to complete the task. Since childhood, I had always felt that something was amiss in those early years of my life, but I had no idea precisely what that absence was. I was fifty-three years old when a colleague at the hospital where I worked, Dr. Radford Tanzer, told me he had once known my father at Harvard Medical School. This chance conversation prompted me to begin my quest to know my father. Since I knew so little about Perry Baird, any information that came my way was of magnified importance. I knew that I had to remain calm, and that I couldn't spend too much time analyzing and reacting to the material. I didn't want my long-held and little-understood emotions to trip me up, so I simply had to move forward with the momentum that the research and writing process required. I came to understand that this approach was going to be the only way I could get my father's story told. And I wasn't getting any younger, so time was of the essence!

Q: What kept you going through the years?
A: My father's own determination was my inspiration. I often thought about those months he spent at Westborough State Hospital, where he endured such atrocious treatments at the hands of his doctors, and yet throughout it all, he continued to write. After reading and rereading the multiple pages of my father's manuscript, it became clear that he wished to have his work published. He wanted to educate members of the public about mental health, in the hope they would become more tolerant of family and

friends who were suffering in similar ways. I became determined to fulfill that wish. My father and I became partners. This gave me enormous strength, and has fueled my will to continue.

Q: Tell me about your father's manuscript—where is it now?
A: After I received the stack of onionskin pages from my cousin in Austin, Texas, I had copies made for myself and my two children. At first, I worked from the original onionskin pages, but as the lead pencil began to come away on my fingertips, I realized just how delicate and valuable these pages were. My father's manuscript had already survived being sent from hospital to hospital during the period of his illness, as well as many decades in a briefcase in my cousin's garage. If I should inadvertently damage the pages it would be a tragedy. From that moment on, I worked only from my copy.

Since that time, the original manuscript has been kept in a large safe deposit box in a bank not far from my home in Vermont. Most of the pages are encased in acid free folders. Before *He Wanted the Moon* was published, there were several times when I had to identify quotes from the manuscript that could be used in the book's final design. The onionskin pages of the original kept in the bank vault are still slightly out of order, so I had to review the entire stack—a process I found very unsettling. One can only read this material so many times.

Arrangements are currently underway to give my father's manuscript to the Harvard Medical Library in the Francis A. Countway Library of Medicine, Center for the History of Medicine.

Q: What was it like to finally see your father's words in print over seventy years after they were written?

A: Frankly, I am still absorbing the magnitude of it all! It is almost too much to process. There were so many junctures when the manuscript could have been mutilated, lost, or completely forgotten. Instead, a magical confluence of events enabled the emergence of my father's work after years of obscurity. I will always be grateful to each person who helped make this possible.

Q: How do your family members feel about the book?

A: They are one hundred percent supportive. For my children and grandchildren, it is a huge relief for them to be able to finally come to grips with our family's secrets. The book has helped all of us to more fully comprehend our heritage and our family's proclivity for mental illness. When *He Wanted the Moon* was first published in New York in February 2015, my children and grandchildren, as well as nieces and nephews, gathered in New York to celebrate. Randy and Karen Baird, my cousins from Texas who had given me my father's manuscript, were also in attendance. The majority of my family had never met my Baird cousins, so it was a very special reunion. For years, there had been silence and separation between my family and our Texas relatives. In New York that day, our family felt whole again. My relatives' enthusiasm for this book continues to inspire me.

Q: What advice do you have for others who want to write about or research their family history?
A: The critical component is passion. It was my passion for uncovering information about my father that helped me to overcome any barriers I met along the way. I began my search with family documents such as baby books and letters, and these primary resources proved invaluable. Although the Internet is a useful tool, traditional libraries can also help in the discovery process. I was fortunate that I applied for my father's medical records before the patient privacy laws (HIPPA) were enacted, which would have made it much more difficult to obtain these crucial documents. I was also very lucky to be able to interview friends and family members about his life, and I'd advise anyone embarking on a similar project to do the same—as soon as possible—particularly when the interview subjects are elderly. If you record these conversations, then you won't have to worry about taking notes and you'll be able to concentrate more fully on the information coming your way. I also found it helpful to keep my findings organized, dated, and in a safe place. A chronology and timeline helped give me a focused overview. It takes time and patience to complete a family history, but with each discovery comes a feeling of accomplishment and the motivation to continue.

Q: What has been the reaction from the medical community to the book?

A: My intention in publishing this book has always been to restore my father's reputation and his place in the medical history. Even though *He Wanted the Moon* has only been available for a short period of time, the reception from the medical community has been incredibly positive. Recently, I was invited to speak about my father and his work at psychiatric grand rounds at a prominent medical school. In the coming months I will give a talk to a group of freshmen medical students. A nationally renowned psychiatrist read *He Wanted the Moon* and desires to get my father's scientific paper republished. After reading the book he wrote to me that, "Your father was a true pioneer who recognized the importance of hypothalamic-pituitary-adreno-cortisol-system-dysregulation in affective disorders. Had he been permitted to pursue his initial studies, his work would have surely accelerated our understanding of the pathophysiology of affective disorders."

Q: As someone with a family member who was mentally ill, what might you suggest for others who are going through similar experiences?

A: Since I am not a professional, these comments come purely from my own experience. I believe awareness and education are the primary tools for understanding and coping with mental illness. Mental illness is a disease, so when family members can be honest and upfront about an individual's sickness, this helps enormously. Conversely, if the illness is kept secret, this only exacerbates the individual's condition and inhibits his or her ability to be treated. As a family member, it is important to seek the guidance of your physician, read as much as you can, and contact a nationally known mental health institution for up-to-date resources. People with mental issues are not necessarily receptive to receiving assistance, so a strong family presence and support may be an essential element of recovery.

Q: How does it feel now that the book has been published? Does it feel as if a new chapter of your life is beginning?

A: When I walk by my local bookstore and see the book displayed, I am still in awe that a major publishing company believed in my father's story. They say that it takes just one editor to champion your work, and it is true. I have such an editor. My father lived out his days hoping his hardships would result in something of worth. His wishes came to fruition with *He Wanted the Moon*. This is a lifetime achievement for both my father and his daughter.

For so many years, I lived under a cloud of secrets. It is a huge relief to be able to continue the rest of my existence with such a clear understanding of my beginnings. There is a freedom that comes with knowledge and this helps mend the fractures of the past. I hope that my experience can inspire others to investigate their past in order to obtain some peace in the years they have ahead.

A Reader's Guide for
He Wanted the Moon

QUESTIONS AND TOPICS FOR DISCUSSION

1. Dr. Baird's manuscript opens in 1944 and yet his story, and the story of his manuscript, spans over a century (including his father's breakdown in 1913 and the publication of *He Wanted the Moon* in 2015). Taking into consideration Dr. Baird's descriptions of his experience being institutionalized, in what ways do you think the stigma of mental illness has and hasn't changed over time?

2. Consider the use of Dr. Baird's manuscript interwoven with his daughter's own pursuit of his story. How does this style affect the way you take in the story? How do you think the reading experience would differ if this were told exclusively in Mimi's voice, or exclusively in her father's voice?

3. Early in the manuscript, Dr. Baird references Mimi Baird as a child. Later, Mimi reflects on

seeing her own name in his story. If you were the author, how would you react to seeing yourself in print from an estranged parent's point of view?

4. Discuss Mimi's mother, Gretta, and how she dealt with her grief. Do you feel compassion for her? Does your understanding of her change as you read about her from Dr. Baird's point of view? From Mimi's? Do you become more sympathetic toward her over the course of the book?

5. Dr. Baird has moments of intense clarity and yet, in many ways, his illness makes him an unreliable narrator, which we see evidence of through medical reports. How do you think this propels his memoir forward? Did you find yourself calling into question his perspective? Did you trust what the doctors reported?

6. Straightjackets are a common trope in depictions of individuals suffering from mental illness. On page thirty-one, Dr. Baird describes part of his ordeal in one: "I lay still for a while, trying to adjust myself to this new and most barbaric treatment. . . . Slowly and methodically I went from knot to knot, untying all kinds of knots, and soon I was almost free. Just as I was about to roll over and free myself entirely, three attendants entered and tied me down again, this time much more securely, leaving me little motion." How does this first-person description affect your view of how

individuals with mental illnesses were treated during the 1940s and 1950s? Do you think straightjackets, and the other extreme treatments Dr. Baird went through, were a necessary evil or perhaps a damaging measure?

7. A painful revelation for Mimi is that Dr. Baird himself believed his illness had a biochemical cause—something that researchers didn't take into account until much later in the century. Moreover, if he had been born just a few years later, he would have benefitted from lithium treatments and Mimi might not have lost her father at such a young age. At the same time, his medical background affords him close relationships with colleagues who possessed an intimate knowledge of his illness. How do you think his stature as a doctor helped and/or hindered him?

8. In chapter eighteen we learn why the book is called *He Wanted the Moon*. Discuss the title and how it applies to Mimi's story and Dr. Baird's story.

9. Throughout Dr. Baird's manuscript, he carefully weighs his desire for escape against his wishes to behave well and show that he is well. In his position, would you try to escape? Why or why not?

10. We hear from Mimi's uncle about how Dr. Baird's lobotomy changed him. Mimi herself discusses the procedure and how it resembled "scrambling eggs" in the brain. How does this

information affect your perception of mental illness and the lengths we've gone to to supposedly "fix" it in this country?

11. Mimi describes the confusion around her father's illness from her perspective as a child, particularly the idea of waiting for him to return. Do you think some of these desires were resolved by the end of the book? Do you think the very act of publishing his work changed her relationship with a man who had been absent for nearly her entire life? How and how not?

12. Mimi learns later in life that her mother had a very similar experience to Mimi with her own father. Yet she handled it in the same way that Mimi's grandmother did. In what ways did Mimi handle it differently? How do familial parallels, and the nature of legacy, play a role in the book?

Resources

MENTAL HEALTH RESOURCES

Our understanding of mental illness has come far since Dr. Baird suffered from it, but asking for help can still be a daunting and confusing process. Today, there are many valuable mental health resources that can make it easier to reach out, a few of which are listed below.

American Psychiatric Association (APA)

http://www.psychiatry.org/   (703) 907-7300

American Psychological Association (APA)

http://www.apa.org/   (800) 374-2721

Anxiety Disorders Association of America (ADAA)

http://www.adaa.org/   (240) 485-1001

American Psychiatric Nurses Association
(APNA)

http://www.apna.org/   (855) 863-2762

National Association of Social Workers
(NASW)

https://www.socialworkers.org/
(800) 742-4089

International Society for Traumatic Stress
Studies (ISTSS)

https://www.istss.org/   (847) 480-9028

National Center for PTSD (NCPTSD)

www.ptsd.va.gov   (802) 296-6300
Veteran's Crisis Helpline: (800) 273-8255
(press 1)

Further Reading

In writing this book, the author found inspiration in others' stories—whether the writers experienced mental illness themselves, loved someone who did, or sought to humanize other sufferers. The works cited below do not comprise a comprehensive list of books that (in some way) informed *He Wanted the Moon*, but serve as a starting point for curious readers.

NONFICTION

Touched with Fire and *An Unquiet Mind*, by Kay Redfield Jamison

Searching for Mercy Street, by Linda Gray Sexton

We Heard the Angels of Madness, by Diane and Lisa Berger

A Mind that Found Itself, by Clifford Whittingham Beers

The Professor and the Madman,
by Simon Winchester

A Mood Apart, by Peter C. Whybrow

The Marriage of Heaven and Hell,
by Peter Dally

Darkness Visible, by William Styron

Girl, Interrupted, by Susanna Kaysen

Memoirs of My Nervous Illness,
by Daniel Paul Schreber

The Noonday Demon and *Far from the Tree,*
by Andrew Solomon

Madness, by Marya Hornbacher

My Age of Anxiety, by Scott Stossel

The Center Cannot Hold, by Elyn R. Saks

The Glass Castle, by Jeanette Walls

The Memory Palace, by Mira Bartok

My Lobotomy, by Howard Dully and
Charles Fleming

Manic, by Terri Cheney

FICTION

The Yellow Wallpaper, by Charlotte Perkins Gilman

The Snake Pit, by Mary Jane Ward

POETRY

Selected Poems, Robert Lowell

Selected Poems, Anne Sexton

For additional Extra Libris content from your other favorite authors and to enter great book giveaways, visit ReadItForward.com/Extra-Libris.

ESSAYS, READER'S GUIDES, AND MORE